Anonymous

**Grandmother's Scrap-Book, or, the Way to do Good**

Designed to Encourage the Highest Religious Attainments Within the....

Anonymous

**Grandmother's Scrap-Book, or, the Way to do Good**
*Designed to Encourage the Highest Religious Attainments Within the....*

ISBN/EAN: 9783337033422

Printed in Europe, USA, Canada, Australia, Japan

Cover: Foto ©Lupo / pixelio.de

More available books at **www.hansebooks.com**

# GRANDMOTHER'S

# SCRAP-BOOK;

OR,

## THE WAY TO DO GOOD.

DESIGNED

TO ENCOURAGE THE HIGHEST RELIGIOUS ATTAINMENTS
WITHIN THE POWER OF MAN.

---

"But to do good, and to communicate, forget not: for with such sacrifices God is well pleased." *Heb.* xiii. 16.
"As we have therefore opportunity, let us do good unto all men." *Gal.* vi. 10.
"For of the abundance of the heart his mouth speaketh." *Luke* vi. 45.

---

BOSTON:
FOR SALE BY CROCKER & BREWSTER,
NO. 51 WASHINGTON STREET.
1869.

# PREFACE.

THE object of this book is to encourage more philanthropy, more confidence in Christ, and perfect faith in prayer.

In order to make any Christian progress, we must first consider the object of this life, — which is, to love and glorify God, and prepare to meet him in heaven. Knowing our duty, we next endeavor to learn Christ's example, and follow in his footsteps. It is the most difficult thing in this life to have our mind fixed on divine things: the care and confusion of this world choke the word. In order to have our thoughts directed more frequently in this direction, let us take the example of Christ. To enable his disciples the better to understand the object of his mission, he directed their thoughts to objects around them. "I am the vine, ye are the branches." "If ye had known who I was, ye would have asked of me, and I would have given you living water."

If we could properly realize this example, and call to mind the objects that meet our eye from day to day, they would preach a sermon to us that would echo back from the eternal world. Before ascending a tree to pluck its golden fruit, let it remind us of the "tree that bears its twelve manner of fruits, and its leaves for the healing of the nation." "Herein is my Father glorified, that ye bear much fruit." "Put not your hand to the plough and look back." "The sower went out to sow." "The field is already white for the harvest." "Ye are the salt of the earth; the wise and foolish builder," &c. If we could carry out suitable thoughts, with the objects that meet the eye from day to day, what a happy progress we should make towards the better land. Look at the encouragement for the believer : —

"Never has it entered into the heart of man to conceive the things that are prepared for them that love God." "Confess your sins unto God, and he is faithful to forgive." " He whose mind is stayed on God is kept in perfect peace." " Every man is rewarded according to what he does." " My yoke is easy and my burden is light." " He that doeth my will shall know of the doctrine." " Know ye that your labor is not in vain in the Lord." " Without faith it is impossible to please . God." " Quench not the Holy Spirit."

Perhaps some may think that they can climb up some other way. "Be not deceived; God is not mocked." He maintains your life. From him all goodness flows. To know him, as revealed in Christ Jesus, is eternal life begun on earth. Acquaint thyself with him, and be at peace; thereby good shall come unto thee. Honor the Son, even as you honor the Father. Receive the Holy Ghost. Devote your life to doing good. Your obligations to do good are perpetual, indissoluble, and mighty. Nothing can remit them. They result from your nature and your relations to God and man. Be humble. If you attain or accomplish any thing, say, "It was not I, but the grace of God." Never forget the judgment-day. Keep it always in view. Frame every action in reference to its unchanging decisions.

If, under the blessing of God, this book should be the means of bringing one benighted, wandering soul to experience the excellency and value of the knowledge of Christ, or of confirming and consoling any that have already believed through grace, the editor will deem his feeble endeavors amply rewarded. It is the sincere wish, and ardent prayer of his heart, that every attempt to diffuse the gospel and its blessings, may be crowned with success by the GREAT HEAD OF THE CHURCH.

# CONTENTS.

|  | PAGE |
|---|---|
| George Washington, | 1 |
| Punctuality, | 3 |
| Battles of the Revolution, | 4 |
| Don't be Selfish, | 6 |
| The Dying Soldier, | 7 |
| A Home Missionary Autobiography, | 10 |
| Dying Advice to Children, | 22 |
| The Sunday School, | 28 |
| The Actress converted, | 29 |
| "No God To-day," | 32 |
| Be Truthful with Children, | 33 |
| Shall I be one of them? | 34 |
| "Live near to God," | 35 |
| The Faithful Mother, | 38 |
| Most Interesting Discovery, | 39 |
| How to make the most of Life, | 40 |
| Serenity in Danger, | 48 |
| The Christian Soldier, | 51 |
| Does the Bible grow old? | 56 |
| The Bible, | 57 |
| Great Reader of the Bible, | 59 |
| "Christ in Me," | 60 |
| Skepticism, | 63 |
| Interesting Incident; or, Bread upon the Waters, | 64 |

## CONTENTS.

| | |
|---|---|
| To Christians preparing for their Summer Excursions, | 67 |
| Sabbath Morning, | 71 |
| "Talk to me of Jesus," | 73 |
| You can never rub it out, | 74 |
| Father, I can't tell a Lie, | 76 |
| "Out of the Mouth of Babes," | 77 |
| Resignation, | 79 |
| Child's Evening Hymn, | 80 |
| God does not forget, he only waits, | 82 |
| The Prodigal's Welcome, | 85 |
| An Example for Boys, | 88 |
| The Way to be saved, | 89 |
| The Wayward Son, | 91 |
| Hard Feelings, | 93 |
| Foretastes of Heaven at the close of Life, | 94 |
| The Christian's Crown, | 100 |
| A Meditation, | 101 |
| Mrs. Hemans, | 105 |
| How Revivals begin, | 106 |
| Excavations in Pompeii, | 108 |
| A Thought for Every Day, | 110 |
| Never give a Kick for a Hit, | 111 |
| Mount Ararat, | 112 |
| Self-Education, | 115 |
| Dr. Franklin as a Money-Lender, | 116 |
| Extent of the Universe, | 117 |
| The Blessedness of being Useful, | 118 |
| Write for Editors, | 122 |
| The most Beautiful Hand, | 127 |
| Ex-President Adams's Opinion of the Bible, | 128 |
| A Sister's Value, | 129 |
| Daily Duties, | 130 |
| The Revival advancing, | 132 |
| Answers to Prayer, | 136 |
| Unbelief, | 138 |
| Humility, | 142 |
| Remember the Children, | 144 |

## CONTENTS.

| | |
|---|---|
| A Father's Counsel, | 145 |
| The Daughters' Lament for the Death of their Mother, | 147 |
| Pouting Jeannie. | 150 |
| The Spirit's teaching, | 152 |
| Pious Mothers, | 158 |
| A Mother's Influence, | 159 |
| Training of Children, | 161 |
| Fifteen Young Men, | 167 |
| "Thou, God, seest Me," | 168 |
| The Absent Daughter, | 169 |
| "Mother is not willing I should go," | 172 |
| A mother's Prayer answered, | 174 |
| The Mother's Faith. — A Fact, | 176 |
| Rev. Warren Burton's Questions, | 179 |
| Regeneration. Written by a Litttle Girl, | 182 |
| A Smile and a Tear, | 185 |
| The Unblessed Meal, | 188 |
| Evening Hymn of a Good Boy, | 189 |
| The Good Shepherd, | 190 |
| Young Men, | 194 |
| A Sermon remembered Eighty-five Years, | 196 |
| How to make Home Attractive, | 198 |
| Domestic Education, | 199 |
| Value of Tract Operations, | 205 |
| The Singing Student Boy, | 206 |
| The Price of a Blessing, and the Means of obtaining it, | 209 |
| An Encouraging Word for the Philanthropist, | 212 |
| Affliction, | 214 |
| Newspapers and their Influence, | 215 |
| The Messenger on the Prairies, | 219 |
| Blessed are they that mourn, | 220 |
| A True Gentleman, | 221 |
| The Angel of Patience, | 222 |
| The Landing at Cape Ann, | 223 |
| An aged Disciple, | 227 |
| Preparation for Death, | 229 |
| Counsel to a Clerk, | 230 |

## CONTENTS.

| | |
|---|---|
| Singular Recovery of a Young Lady given up to die, | 231 |
| A Smart Old Man, | 233 |
| A Man killed by a Lion at Astley's London Amphitheatre, | 234 |
| Commercial Value of Honesty, | 237 |
| What is God? | 239 |
| The Tract Society and the Army, | 241 |
| The War, | 242 |
| A Sea-Captain's Opinion of Novels, | 244 |
| A Useful Hint to Young Men, | 246 |
| Pray for Editors, | 247 |
| Be in earnest, | 248 |
| The Colporteur's Treat, | 249 |
| Influence of the Messenger, | 250 |
| One Voyage More, | 251 |
| The Family Rods, | 254 |
| The Mother's Last Lesson, | 258 |
| Destitution in New York, | 261 |
| Power of Religion, | 262 |
| Words Fitly Spoken, | 266 |
| Pride, | 267 |
| The Novel Reader, | 270 |
| Fashionable Call, | 273 |
| The Best Sermon, | 275 |
| Daniel Webster on Preaching, | 277 |
| The Ministry we need, | 281 |
| Encouragement to the Afflicted, | 284 |
| Old South Chapel Prayer-Meeting, and its Influence, | 286 |
| Specific Prayer, | 293 |
| The Bible, | 297 |
| The Bible in Turkey, | 299 |
| The Old Family Bible, | 300 |
| Believe, | 301 |
| The Bible and its Influence, | 302 |
| Why I attend Church on Rainy Sabbaths, | 305 |
| Medicine for the Disconsolate, | 308 |
| Profanity, | 309 |
| Adulterated Liquors, | 310 |
| Scene in a Grog-shop, | 312 |

CONTENTS. xi

| | |
|---|---|
| A Visit to the Tombs, Court Square, | 313 |
| Increase of Crime, and its Remedy, | 317 |
| The Little Ones at Prayer, | 324 |
| Faith in God, | 326 |
| The State of Probation, | 327 |
| Eternity, | 328 |
| Divinity of Christ, | 329 |
| Experience, | 330 |
| From Lavater, | 331 |
| A Fragment from Andrew Fuller, | 332 |
| Two Classes of Christians, | 333 |
| "My Life has been a Failure," | 334 |
| What pleases God will please Me, | 336 |
| Worthy of Respect, | 337 |
| Anecdote of Daniel Webster, | 338 |
| Be Social, | 339 |
| In the Garden, | 340 |
| Cheerfulness, | 342 |
| The Life-Preserver, | 343 |
| Doubt from Inactivity, | 352 |
| How to be a Man, | 353 |
| Causes of Failures in Business, | 354 |
| Selections from Scripture, | 355 |
| A short Sermon on Manliness, | 358 |
| Trees and Flowers, | 359 |
| Think, | 360 |
| Wear a Smile, | 361 |
| Do Good, | 362 |
| The Prevention of Crime, | 363 |
| God knows it All, | 367 |
| How to Live, | 369 |
| The Golden City, | 371 |
| Prayer, | 373 |
| Whitefield's Experience, | 376 |
| A Word from Old South Chapel, | 378 |
| Every Man's Life a Plan of God, | 380 |
| A Word to Mothers, | 381 |
| Conclusion, | 382 |

# GRANDMOTHER'S SCRAP-BOOK;

OR,

## THE WAY TO DO GOOD.

### GEORGE WASHINGTON.

THERE are few left among us who can boast the remembrance of having seen the living Washington. The recollections of him by Rev. Dr. Ely, of Monson, which we recently published, have been widely copied, and have stirred up the youthful memories of other ancient and venerable men. Father Boylston, of the Amherst (N. H.) Cabinet, — an honored native of our town, — recalls seeing Washington here in 1789, when a boy.

"Washington was on a visit to the arsenal, where his dignified and commanding appearance attracted the observance of all, especially the boys. His cocked hat, from under which protruded the staid ear-locks, and the stately tie-behind, powdered white as snow, in the ancient style, are perfectly recollected, and are ever brought vividly to mind whenever viewing the likenesses of him representing him in that costume. As he walked round among the stacks of glistening small arms and the grisly big guns in the 'public stores,' he was closely beset by the boys, as is their way, intensely gazing in his face, eagerly catching every word, and gleam of his benignant countenance, for future remembrance. As an appendage to the cavalcade which escorted him, the boys rode on canes and sticks, following the procession, delighted as any in their part of the grand exhibition, shouting, 'We've seen him! We've seen George Washington!' There were present in that procession many revolutionary characters, in their cocked hats and other dress peculiar to the times."

PUNCTUALITY. — Washington was a minuteman. An accurate clock in the entry at Mount Vernon controlled the movements of the family. At his dinner parties, he allowed five minutes for difference of watches, and then waited for no one. If members of Congress came at a late hour, his simple apology was, " Gentlemen, we are too punctual for you;" or, "Gentlemen, I have a cook who never asks whether the company has come, but whether the hour has come." Nobody ever waited for General Washington. He was always five minutes before the time; and if the parties he had engaged to meet were not present at the season appointed, he considered the engagement cancelled, and would leave the place, and refuse to return.

IMPORTANCE OF LAUGHING. — Dr. Ray, superintendent of the Butler Hospital for the Insane, says, " A hearty laugh is more desirable for mental health than any exercise of the reasoning faculties."

SHORT SPEECHES. — "I served," says Jefferson, "with General Washington, in the legislature of Virginia, before the Revolution, and during it with Dr. Franklin, in Congress. I never heard either of them speak ten minutes at a time, nor to any but the main point which was to decide the question. They laid their shoulders to the great points, knowing that the little ones would follow of themselves."

## BATTLES OF THE REVOLUTION.

### LOSS OF LIFE THEREBY.

A CORRESPONDENT of the Norfolk Herald has taken the pains to compile the following table, showing the comparative losses of life sustained in the battles of the Revolution. He says that he may have made some trifling errors, but that the statistics are mainly correct to the figure. The table should be preserved for future reference : —

OR, THE WAY TO DO GOOD. 5

| Battles. | British loss. | Amer. loss. |
|---|---|---|
| Lexington, April 19, 1775, | 273 | 84 |
| Bunker Hill, June 17, 1775, | 1064 | 453 |
| Flatbush, August 12, 1776, | 400 | 200 |
| White Plains, August 26, 1776, | 400 | 400 |
| Trenton, December 25, 1776, | 1000 | 9 |
| Princeton, January 5, 1777, | 400 | 100 |
| Hubbardstown, August 17-18, 1777, | 800 | 800 |
| Bennington, August 16, 1777, | 800 | 100 |
| Brandywine, September 11, 1777, | 500 | 1100 |
| Stillwater, September 17, 1777, | 600 | 350 |
| Germantown, October 4, 1777, | 600 | 1200 |
| Saratoga, October 17, 1777 (surrendered), | 5752 | |
| Red Hook, October 22, 1777, | 500 | 32 |
| Monmouth, June 26, 1778, | 400 | 130 |
| Rhode Island, August 27, 1778, | 260 | 241 |
| Briar Creek, March 30, 1779, | 13 | 400 |
| Stoney Point, July 15, 1779, | 600 | 100 |
| Camden, August 16, 1779, | 375 | 610 |
| King's Mountain, October 1, 1780, | 950 | 96 |
| Cowpens, January 17, 1781, | 800 | 72 |
| Guilford Court House, March 15, 1781, | 532 | 400 |
| Hobkirk Hills, April 25, 1781, | 400 | 460 |
| Eutaw Springs, September, 1781, | 1000 | 550 |
| Yorktown, October 19, 1781 (surrendered), | 7072 | |

Don't be selfish. — There is no virtue which is more respected than unselfishness; and hence we find the man who attains the greatest popularity in this world is not he who amasses great wealth or stands high in the temple of fame, but it is he who, like our Great Master, went about continually doing good, and by his philanthropic exertions has effected a measure whereby the hungry are fed, the naked clothed, and spiritual provision made for those who have been less favorably situated than himself.

How few think of it. — A stranger once stopped a gentleman in London, and abruptly asked him, "Did you ever thank God for your reason?" "I don't know that I ever did," was the reply. "Do it quickly then," said the stranger, "for I have lost mine."

Millennium. — During this period, it will not be needful for persons to engage in manual labor more than will be required by the health and vigor of the body.

## THE DYING SOLDIER.

It was just after the battle of Williamsburg, where hundreds of our brave fellows had fallen, never to bear arms again in their country's cause, and where hundreds more were wounded, that a soldier came to the tent of a delegate of the Christian Commission, and said, "Chaplain, one of our boys is badly wounded, and wants to see you right away."

"Hurriedly following the soldier," says the delegate, "I was taken to the hospital, and led to a bed upon which lay a noble young soldier. He was pale and blood-stained from a terrible wound above the temple. I saw at a glance that he had but a few hours to live upon earth. Taking his hand, I said to him, 'Well, my brother, what can I do for you?'

"The poor dying soldier looked up in my face, and placing his finger where his hair was stained with his blood, he said, 'Chaplain, cut a big lock from here for mother! for *mother*, mind, chaplain.' I hesitated to do it. He said, 'Don't be afraid, chaplain, to disfigure my hair; it's for mother, and nobody will come to see me in the deadhouse to-morrow.'

"I did as he requested me. 'Now, chaplain,' said the dying man, 'I want you to kneel down by me, and return thanks to God.' For what? I asked. 'For giving me such a mother. O chaplain, she is a good mother; her teachings comfort and console me now. And, chaplain, thank God that by his grace I am a Christian. O, what would I do now, if I wasn't a Christian? I know that my Redeemer liveth. I feel that his finished work has saved me. And, chaplain, thank God for giving me dying grace. He has made my dying bed feel soft as downy pillows are. Thank him for the promised home in glory. I'll soon be there — there, where there is no war, nor sorrow, nor desolation, nor death, —

where I'll see Jesus, and be forever with the Lord.'

"I knelt by the dying man, and thanked God for the blessings he had bestowed upon him — the blessings of a good mother, a Christian hope, and dying grace to bear testimony to God's faithfulness.

"Shortly after the prayer he said, 'Goodby, chaplain; if you ever see mother, tell her it was all well!'"

---

VENTILATE YOUR BED-ROOMS. — It is stated that a bird suspended near the top of a curtained bedstead, in which people are sleeping, will generally be found dead in the morning, from the impure air generated by their respiration. Small, close sleeping rooms are often as dangerous as the curtained bedstead.

When the heart is pure, there is hardly any thing that can mislead the understanding.

## A HOME MISSIONARY AUTOBIOGRAPHY.

I LOVE my missionary field, for the reason which, I hope, dear sir, you will excuse me for giving; although, by giving it, I must give something of my early history, which will partake somewhat of the nature of egotism, and be also quite unusual in a missionary report. The first two cents I ever remember of possessing all at once, was when I was about ten years old. On the first Sabbath of June, there was to be a collection taken up for foreign missions. The Tuesday following was then the great spring holiday in Vermont, i. e., the " June training." If I gave my two cents to foreign missions, I must go without my gingerbread on training-day. It was a *great* sacrifice to give *my all*, but when the hat came round, in they dropped. Training-day came, and boys of my age, who gave nothing on the Sabbath to send the gospel to the heathen, had their two, three, and six cents' worth of gingerbread. I began to relent, till taunted by one of my playmates, with what he called my " folly," in giving my money to the heathen that I knew nothing about. This aroused all my consciousness of having done right, and revived the latent notion, previously entertained, that, somehow, those two cents would come back to me in something far better than gingerbread, and far more enduring. The regrets were all gone; the day passed pleasantly, though I confess I *was* hungry before night; but never was a basin of bread and milk eaten with a keener relish than was mine that night, sharpened as my appetite had been by the day's fasting. During the winter of 1815 I read the report of a missionary who had labored a few months in the northern parts of New Hampshire and Maine. The account he gave of the moral desolations through which he had passed drew tears to my eyes. Though not then possessing any personal interest in religion, O, how I wished that God would convert me, that I too might become a missionary, and labor amidst such moral desolation. During the following year there was a gentle outpouring of the Holy Spirit, especially upon the youth and children. I was the only boy in the part of the town where my parents resided who became interested in that revival. I hope that I then became a subject of converting and regenerating grace. I immediately began to revolve in my mind the question how I might get an education, so that I might preach Christ and him crucified in some of the destitute portions of our country, but especially in some poor place, where no one with a more thorough education than I could ever expect to acquire, would feel willing, or be in duty bound, to stop. I thought myself a very dull scholar, for I had had a very poor chance for schooling, owing to the fact that my father, who was a mechanic, was deeply in debt, with a large family to support, and therefore needed my work in the shop. This often took me from the winter school more than half of the time. I was, therefore, in great fear that I could not learn.

In the spring, a Sabbath school was commenced. I entered the school, determined to solve the question, whether I could commit to memory my Sabbath-school lessons with sufficient ease to justify me in entering upon a course of study for the ministry. Each child in the Sabbath school was expected to commit to memory as many verses in the New Testament as they could, from week to week, and to recite them to the teacher on the Sabbath. With great effort I succeeded in committing, perfectly, to memory nineteen verses of the fifth chapter of Matthew, as my first Sabbath-school lesson. When haying came, I took my Testament with my scythe and rake to the field, read a verse, then laid my Testament down at the end of the swath, and repeated it over till I returned to it. Usually, reading a verse once or twice, would fix it in my memory. Once, during haying, I had a whole rainy day to myself. With what I committed to memory in the field, and during that glorious rainy day, I was able to recite nine whole chapters, and fourteen verses of the tenth chapter, as my Sabbath-school lesson the next Sabbath. The whole was repeated with ease, and with prompting in but a single instance. The effect of this, in itself trifling circumstance, was to convince me that I could learn as well as others, could I only have the time for study. O, how my poor heart leaped for joy while I reasoned thus with myself: "If, under such disadvantages, I could commit to memory so many chapters in the Bible, surely I can commit to memory the English grammar, and the Latin and the Greek grammars too, only give me the time!"

Thus, the first great difficulty was removed. I could learn. But could I command the time and the means? And would God accept of me? These questions troubled me. About this time an agent for Foreign Missions came into the place, and calling on the families, took a subscription for his object, to be paid in two months. I subscribed thirty-seven and a half cents. This was a larger sum than I had ever possessed at a time. How was I to get it? I contrived a thousand ways; set traps for muskrats, but caught only one tail and two feet. I would borrow it; but how pay the borrowed money? The two months were nearly gone, and I almost began to despair, when Judge L——, who owned a farm near father's, called at the shop, and requested him to let one of his boys pull a yard of turnips, and take them up to his house, a mile and a half distant. I begged the privilege of doing the job by moonlight, that I might take the money and pay my subscription to the Foreign Mission cause.

Father gave his permission; and never was the same amount of work done with a lighter heart or in a shorter time. I received for my work two old-fashioned pistareens (twenty-cent pieces) — forty cents! The same work could not be obtained now short of a dollar and a half. But I was rich. I could redeem my pledge to the Missionary Society, and have two cents left. No, dear sir, never did one of your merchant princes have more real joy, when, as the result of some shrewd speculation, or fortunate investment, or from the timely return of a richly-freighted vessel, he found himself enriched by additional thousands, than I felt when I had those two shining pieces of silver in my hand. And for two reasons — I could pay my subscription; but chiefly, because I saw, or thought I saw, in that little incident, the Providence which would supply me with the means for study. Nor was I mistaken. But would God accept of me, and put me in the ministry? Two points had been gained. I could learn; and I thought I saw upon what I might safely rely for means with which to pay for my education. But was I called of God, as was Aaron, to the ministry? This question was soon after solved on this wise. An agent of the Education Society visited the place. He presented, in glowing colors, the amazing destitution of our own country and the world, and the necessity of a greater number of educated ministers of all grades of intellect. He said he wanted men and money, but young men more than money. A collection was taken up. I had not even two cents then. As the box passed me, I thought, as Peter said, to the lame man, " Silver and gold have I none, but such as I have I will give." I gave myself.

I went from the meeting, and told my excellent mother what I had done. The tear that stood in her eye told me of her deep interest in the act of her boy; while, with a quivering lip, she informed me how she, too, though ignorant of the struggles of my mind, had responded to the following question of the agent: " Is there not some mother present, who, though she may have no money to give, has what is better, a son of the covenant, concerning whom she has hope, whom she will give up to the work of the ministry for Christ's sake, and for the sake of a dying world?" Her response was, "Yes, here is my son; take him for any post, however obscure, if so be that he may tell the story of a Saviour's dying love to perishing sinners." Here, under a mother's eye, and encouraged by her tears and prayers, the third, and last question (to my mind) was solved. While seated by her in the house of God, my mother had given me, and I had given myself, to Christ, at the same moment, and for the same purpose, i. e., to preach the gospel in some poor place, where others of stronger minds, and with better education than I could hope to obtain, would neither be willing, or feel it to be their duty, to labor. This done, I could no longer hesitate.

And it was surprising how soon the way was opened for me to commence my studies. True, it was with many disadvantages, and in a way I would never advise a poor student to take. I had to work from four to six hours a day for my board. For a while I rung the bell at the academy for my tuition, boarding at home, a mile and a half from the school. I then took my box of cold food to my room near the academy, and studied always till after nine, and often till twelve o'clock at night, before returning home. This was rather a cold job, especially in the winters. I had to cut wood for three fires, and take care of the barn in the morning. To do this, I often rose at four o'clock, and cut my wood by lantern light. After nearly four years' labor and study after this manner, and with no assistance, except the payment of my board for a single term, and tuition for four or five terms at the academy, I found myself prepared to enter college one year in advance.

\* \* \* \* \*

On leaving the seminary, and after four months spent as city missionary in Boston, I entered the service of the Massachusetts Home Missionary Society. At that time B——, where I went to labor, was a most forbidding field.

The society was small, and without a meeting-house which they could control. Opposition was rife and implacable. The pulpit Bible was stolen from the meeting-house, and hid for months in a stone wall; my horse was taken from my barn and rode in the night; the barn doors thrown open, and cattle let into my garden, and among my apple trees. Though my ministry there was short and full of trials, it was not without important results; for the church was purified of its lifeless and heretical members, and *doubled* in numbers from the fruits of a precious revival; and, at great pecuniary sacrifice on my part, a neat and sufficiently large meeting-house was built. And it has been the occasion of no small degree of pleasure that I have learned that *all* the members of the Sabbath school which I gathered there, except one, have since been brought into the church. That Sabbath school numbered thirty-nine scholars.

In another feeble church, where this brother has labored, twenty-four were added the first year, fruits of a previous revival, and another house of worship was built; and in the present field of his labors, there is a very encouraging advancement of the kingdom of Christ. Enduring hardness, as a good soldier, fits the ministers of Christ for eminent usefulness.

CHRISTIAN TREASURY OF PERSONAL DUTY. — "*Know* thyself." *Reverence* thyself. "*Deny* thyself." *Govern* thyself. "Abhor and flee from the *appearance* of evil." Guard the senses. Avoid all occasions of impurity in heart. Eat and drink " to the glory of God." Eat to live, rather than live to eat. Be careful of health. Avoid repletion.

A SAILOR'S GRATITUDE. — We have received three dollars from a sailor, who experienced so much benefit from reading the tract entitled " Tom and Harry," that he felt called upon to do something towards extending the circulation of tracts.

## DYING ADVICE TO CHILDREN.

SOLEMN and impressive was the scene, as I stood by the bedside of a dying father. Friends and neighbors were assembled, awaiting with trembling anxiety the last expiring breath which was every moment expected. Already had he remained several hours in a sleep or stupor, from which it was supposed he would never again awake to consciousness. All were silent; not even a whisper was uttered; no sound was heard in that sick room but the short and labored breathing of the dying man, when, to the astonishment of every beholder, he suddenly aroused, almost as from the sleep of death, and inquired for his children. He said, " Let them come in, in the order of their ages."

With weeping eyes, and solemn, slow, and silent footsteps, his five children approached his bedside, and there stood, with trembling limbs and fast falling tears, while in the most earnest and affectionate manner he took each successively by the hand, and addressed them in the following words, commencing with the youngest, a boy of six, and proceeding regularly to the eldest, a youth of fifteen. His sentences were short, but distinctly uttered, and with an ardor, pathos, and solemnity, never to be forgotten. Taking his hand, he said, " My dear Willie, your father is soon to die. You are too young to realize it now, but I wish you to remember what I say to you. Try to be a good boy. Give your heart to the Saviour. Be obedient to your mother, and kind to your brother and sisters. Never play with wicked boys. Keep all God's commands; especially remember the Sabbath day, to keep it holy. Farewell."

" And now, my dear little Arabella," said he, taking her hand, " I am going to leave you, and then you will see my face no more. I want you to love and serve the blessed Saviour. Pray to God to give you a new heart, for although you are young, you have a sinful heart, that needs to be renewed by the Holy Spirit. Endeavor to follow the example of those pious children, of whom you read in your Sabbath-school books. Lay up your treasure in heaven, and prepare to meet me there. Farewell." To Frances he said, as he took her hand, " My dear daughter, you weep because you see me dying, but I expect to go to heaven, and I wish you to meet me there. Remember that you, too, must die, and you know not how soon. It becomes you, then, to make your peace with God now, that you may be prepared for sickness and death whenever it comes. Make the Saviour your friend, and he will take care of you while you live, and support and comfort you in the hour of death. You see how he sustains me in this dying hour, and I trust will take me safe to heaven. Farewell."

"My dear Isabella," said he, clasping her hand, " you are soon to be without any father on earth; put your trust in your Father in heaven. He is able to take care of you, and do for you all that you need. Be kind and obedient to your mother. Be much in her society, for she will be very desolate when I am gone. Assist her all in your power in teaching and taking care of the younger children: You must be economical, and remember that all your wants cannot be supplied. Set not too high a value on the things of this world. Be sure to seek an interest in the Saviour, and 'lay up a treasure in heaven.' Farewell."

"Henry, my dear son, I have many things to say to you, but my strength is almost gone. Remember the instructions I have given you heretofore, and endeavor to profit by them. Be very kind and obedient to your mother. As you are the oldest, it will be natural for her to expect some assistance from you. Disappoint not her hopes. She will have you *all* to care for and support; try to lighten her cares what you can. Ever cherish a kind regard for her feelings. Consult her in regard to every important measure. As your time and attention have been devoted to study, I think you had better make an effort to go through college. In regard to that, however, consult Mr. O.; he will advise you. Spend your evenings at home. Improve well your time. Whether you study or work, be diligent. Above all things, make your peace with God now; and then, if your life is spared, you may do good in the world. Farewell."

"And now, my dear children, I must leave you. I shall never more return to you, but you must prepare to come to me. Seek the Lord *now;* defer it not another night, not another hour. Some of you have had serious impressions. O, cherish such impressions. Think not that you are too young to seek religion. Think of Miss D.; she was younger than some of you, only nine years old when she gave her heart to the Saviour, and united with the church; and see how she has been growing in grace ever since! and what a bright and shining Christian she is now! How she loves her Saviour, and delights in doing good!

"Ever read the Bible daily, and regard what it teaches. Let there be no discord among you. Dwell together in love, and as you encircle the family altar from day to day, be solemn and devout. I leave you with no legacy but my prayers, and the precious promises of the Bible. You are to follow my body to the cold and silent grave, and you cannot conceive, nor I describe, the desolateness you will feel when you return and find that you have no *father*. But God has said he will be a Father of the fatherless. He feeds the young ravens when they cry, and he will feed and take care of you, if you put your trust in him, and choose him for your Father."

These were the last words he uttered, except, " Come, Lord Jesus, come quickly."

THE SECRET OF HAPPINESS. — We can be truly happy but in proportion as we are the instruments of promoting the happiness of others.

## THE SUNDAY SCHOOL.

**BY THE REV. LUTHER LEE.**

'Mid all the various walks of life,
   No joy is found so sweet,
As when away from scenes of strife,
   In Sunday school we meet.

There truth divine our hearts expand,
   Our bosoms feel delight;
O, what a cheerful, happy band!
   O, what a lovely sight!

We here peruse the sacred page,
   And oft with wonder pause,
And then with earnestness engage,
   To learn Jehovah's laws.

And when we chant the song of praise,
   All think and feel the same
As we our infant voices raise,
   And bless the Saviour's name.

## THE ACTRESS CONVERTED.

A DRESSMAKER had exhausted her work, and begun to be sorely pressed for fear she should be in want. All this is of very recent date. She looked about in vain for employment and bread. So she went to her heavenly Father, and told him all her case, and begged that he would send her employment, in humble, fervent prayer.

Soon after she had offered up her humble supplications to God, an actress came in, with a large amount of work to be done; for which she was willing to pay a very liberal price. It was altering, fitting, and making dresses for the stage. She wanted the work done immediately, and a full compensation would be paid at once. She urged despatch.

The poor, pious sewing girl was in great perplexity. She knew not what to do. She needed employment, for she had prayed for it. But was it right for her to earn money by working upon dresses to be worn in the demoralizing business of the stage? That was the question. So she frankly told this young actress her difficulties and perplexities, and proposed to her to remain in her room, while she kneeled down and asked the direction of God in prayer. She kneeled accordingly, and poured out her heart to her heavenly Father, and besought him to reveal to her what she ought to do. She had not proceeded long in her prayer before the actress came and kneeled down beside her, and, throwing her arms around her neck, exclaimed, "You need not pray any longer about the dresses,—I don't care any thing about the dresses,—but, O, pray for me, for I am a poor, miserable, wicked girl!"

The dressmaker *did* pray for her—the actress—with strong crying and tears. She poured out her heart in prayer to God that he would have mercy upon the actress, and bring her at once, then and there, to embrace Jesus Christ, as the Way, the Light, the Life. And she did embrace him truly and heartily. She resolved to renounce her profession at once, and there, on the spot, to begin a new life. She was under contract to play an engagement in Philadelphia. She sat down at once, and wrote to the manager as follows: "I can no longer *play* for you, but I will *pray* for you."

---

WHICH HAS THE ADVANTAGE? — Dr. Hall, of New York, in his Journal of Health, says, "We believe a man feels as happy after a plain dinner as after a luxurious one ; certain are we that he sleeps sounder that night, and feels the better for it all next day; all the advantage to the luxurious liver is the transient passage down the throat."

CHANGE of time, like change of place, introduces men to new associates, and gives many persons an opportunity to become respected, by outliving those who know them when they were not respectable.

## "NO GOD TO-DAY."

Anna was the child of prayerless parents. The family met in the morning, gathered round the table, spread with bounties from a loving Father's hand, with no acknowledgment of the gracious Giver. And so they passed the day, and lay down at night, with no thanks for the day's mercies, no committal of all to Him who never slumbers nor sleeps.

At length there came a pious uncle to spend a few weeks with them. During his stay he was invited to ask a blessing at meals, and to conduct family worship.

The morning after his departure the family were at the table, and about to commence their meal without a blessing, when little Anna, who sat next her father, looked up and said, "No God to-day, papa." The child's touching rebuke went straight to the father's heart, and, like an arrow from the Almighty, rankled there until he found peace in Jesus, and began to acknowledge God at meals, at the family altar, and in all his ways.

---

BE TRUTHFUL WITH CHILDREN. — Some people tell lies to children, with a view of enjoying a laugh at their credulity. This is to make a mock at sin, and they are fools who do it. The tendency in a child to believe whatever it is told, is of God, for good. It is lovely. It seems a shadow of primeval innocence glancing by. We should reverence a child's simplicity. Touch it only with truth. Be not the first to quench that lovely truthfulness by falsehoods.

WORTH HEEDING. — "Do all the good you can in the world, and make as little noise about it as possible," was one of Dr. Nettleton's excellent maxims.

THE most valuable knowledge comes from common experience, and lodges not in the memory, but in the understanding.

### SHALL I BE ONE OF THEM?

How divinely full of glory and pleasure shall that hour be, when all the millions of mankind that have been redeemed by the blood of the Lamb of God, shall meet together and stand around him, with every tongue and every heart full of joy and praise! How astonishing will be the glory and the joy of that day, when all the saints shall join together in one common song of gratitude and everlasting thankfulness to their Redeemer! With what unknown delight and inexpressible satisfaction shall all that are saved from the ruins of sin and hell address the Lamb that was slain, and rejoice in his presence!

---

THE exemption of women in the United States from out-door toil has some advantages, but both sexes have probably less strength of constitution in consequence.

## "LIVE NEAR TO GOD."

A FAIR young matron lay on her death-bed. It was in one of our Western cities, far away from the home of her childhood, parents, brother, and sisters. The world was fast receding, — the faces of loved ones around her were becoming more and more shadowy, — when some one bent down to her ear, and said, "And what message have you for your distant sisters and brother?" "Tell them," said the dying woman, "tell them to live near to God."

When this last message from the departed sister reached the survivors, it seemed like a voice from the tomb, — "Live near to God!" — "live near to God!" When vexing cares came, and the world occupied too large a place in the heart, the dying sister's warning asserted its right to be heard, — "Live near to God!"

How full of meaning are these words. Those who obey them need not fear to die.

But comparatively little stress is laid in the Bible upon the *death* of believers. If they *live near to God*, they are numbered with the righteous.

Baalim was willing " to die the death of the righteous," but he was not willing to live their life of nearness to God.

Well may those who live near to God not fear to die. Shall not the King of Terrors be shorn of his power if God is near? If on the ill-fated Central America there was one man who had lived near to God, — and there was one whom the writer knew, — was he not supported in that dreadful hour? He sent no dying message to his friends; there was no one to convey it. But he had lived near to God, and, no doubt, God was with him in his extremity. Amid those wild and terrible waters he could discern his Father's chariot, which was to convey him home.

If we live near to God, we never need complain of loneliness. He sticketh closer than a brother. How lonely does the pathway of some of our race appear! Some have neither father, mother, wife, child, brother, or sister. But if they live near to God, do not tell me of their loneliness. They hear a voice the worldling cannot hear — whispers of a love so broad and deep that it will take all eternity to comprehend it. We need God near us. We need him every day. We need the restraints of his presence, the comfort of his love; his sympathy, his wisdom to direct us. Happy are they who feel God near and dear to them; who have him for a constant guest in their hearts.

A SINGULAR REMEDY. — A refractory patient in an English lunatic asylum, who was in the habit of tearing his clothes into shreds, was dressed in a new suit. He had been a tailor, and either from an appreciation of their value, or from being touched by this mark of attention, spared them whole, and from that time rapidly recovered, ascribing his cure to the good effects of a new suit of clothes.

## THE FAITHFUL MOTHER.

A MOTHER whose children all bore the fruits of early piety, on being asked what the secret of her influence was, answered thus: "While my children were infants on my lap, as I washed them, I raised my heart to God that he would wash them in that blood which cleanseth from all sin. As I dressed them in the morning, I asked my heavenly Father to clothe them with the robe of Christ's righteousness. As I provided them food, I prayed that God would feed their souls with the bread of heaven, and give them to drink of the water of life. When I have prepared them for the house of God, I have pleaded that their bodies might be fit temples for the Holy Ghost to live in. When they left me for the week-day school, I followed their infant footsteps with prayer, that their path through life might be like that of the just, which shineth more and more unto the perfect day. And as I put them to bed, the silent breathing of my soul has been, that their heavenly Father would take them to his embrace and fold them in his paternal arms."

MOST INTERESTING DISCOVERY. — The Rev. Dr. McCrie, in his antiquarian explorations of London, has discovered the Minutes of the Westminster Assembly, in manuscript, extending over the whole period of its sittings. Dr. Lee, Principal of Edinburgh University, believed they had been destroyed by fire. They are now found in the Episcopal Library of Sion College, in the city, where Presbytery, in its brief, palmy days, had its headquarters.

THE French say, "He who has a good son-in-law, has gained a son; he who has a bad one, has lost a daughter."

THOSE who have the fewest ungratified wants often have the most ungratified wishes.

## HOW TO MAKE THE MOST OF LIFE.

On this winged hour eternity depends. Both the kind and degree of eternal retribution will be determined by present conduct. "Whatsoever a man soweth, that shall he also reap." How, then, shall a man *make the most of life?*

*Know thyself.* Self-knowledge is first in order. The prodigal first "came to himself," and then to his father. The royal Psalmist says, "I thought on *my* ways, and turned my feet unto *thy* testimonies." If you would gain correct knowledge of yourself, you must receive the scriptural account of human nature as true of *you.*

*Know God.* He maintains your life. From him all goodness flows. To know him, as revealed in Christ Jesus, is eternal life begun on earth. Acquaint thyself with him, and be at peace; thereby good shall come unto thee. Honor the Son even as you honor the Father.

Receive the Holy Ghost. To the sacred Three in One consecrate all you have, and are, and hope for.

*Devote your life to doing good.* Your obligations to do good are perpetual, indissoluble, and mighty. Nothing can remit them. They result from your nature and your relations to God and man. In doing good,—

*Discern the nature of things.* Make a careful selection. Squander nothing on unworthy objects, or in unworthy pursuits. Learn to judge of both men and things.

*Watch for opportunities.* Henry Martyn, with all his zeal, says he lost, through inattention, the best opportunity for usefulness which he had for many months in India. "O, that our heads were waters (exclaims Cotton Mather), because they have been so dry of all thoughts to do good. O, that our eyes were a fountain of tears, because they have looked so little for occasions to do good." "As we have therefore *opportunity*, let us do good unto all men."

*Let your ability be the rule of your efforts.* "Get all you can, save all you can, give all you can," do all you can. "If there be first a willing mind, it is accepted according to what a man hath, and not according to what he hath not." "Withhold not good from them to whom it is due, when it is in the power of thy hand to do it."

*Never quit certainty for hope.* Never abandon a sure way of doing good for some doubtful scheme. Conform your plans to the rule of God's providence and the dictates of a sober mind. Beware of the habit of originating devices which you do not intend to execute.

*Persevere.* When you have made a good beginning, do not think the work done. Call not a commencement the completion. "Let not him that girdeth on his harness boast himself, as he that putteth it off." Have "long patience," and you shall have "precious fruits."

*Be impartial.* Never favor one good cause or object of charity to the prejudice of another. It was a shame for the early Christians to wrangle about the comparative merits of Paul, Apollos, and Cephas. They all had excellent gifts and more excellent graces. 'Tis a mark of folly, yea, it is a sin, to undervalue objects merely because we are not engaged in promoting them. Therefore, encourage whatever promises substantial good.

*Defer not.* To assign to the future what God assigns to the present is very hazardous. One would not give any, until he could give a large sum; when he had a large part of the desirable sum, he lost it by fire. Another deferred for one hour a warning which he intended to give an unconverted friend; at the end of the hour the unconverted man was in eternity. "Say not unto thy neighbor, Go, and come again, and to-morrow I will give, when thou hast it by thee." To-morrow is not thine.

*Act from principle.* What you do, do not from persuasion, or fancy, or ostentation, or to avoid importunity. You have a rational soul. Make use of it. Be fully persuaded and firmly established in good *principles.*

*Live by rule.* Be systematic in your charities and efforts. If there be irregularity in your life, let it come from the overflowing of your benevolence breaking over a well-constructed system of usefulness.

*Be hearty in all your labors.* Let not your head, and hands, and tongue be busy, and your heart idle. Results, by their greatness, will surprise the truly engaged, while the double minded will wonder that so little good is done. When the walls of Jerusalem went up rapidly, it was because "the people had a mind to build." "The sluggard desireth, and hath nothing."

*Enlist others.* "Iron sharpeneth iron, so a man sharpeneth the countenance of his friend." "Two are better than one. Woe to him who is alone when he falleth. A threefold cord is not quickly broken. One shall chase a thousand, and two shall put ten thousand to flight." Despise not the services of any *in their appropriate sphere.* A little captive maid knew more about the man of God in Palestine than did the king of Israel, and was the means of saving her master Naaman.

*Be not unmindful of little things.* Nothing is of little importance which possesses, even in its results, the attributes of eternity. Despise not the day of small things. "Sands form the mountains; minutes make the year."

*Spare not thyself.* The greatest good is only accomplished by the greatest pains. "He that soweth sparingly shall reap also sparingly; he that soweth bountifully shall reap also bountifully."

*Maintain cheerfulness.* The demon of melancholy unnerves religious effort. Be joyful in the Lord, for the joy of the Lord is strength. Rarely will you find a better motto than this: "*Serve God, and be cheerful.*"

*Be of good courage.* In the Christian course, cowardice alone is the loss of nearly every victory. It is needless; it is wicked. "The voice that rolls the stars along spake all the promises."

*Be not faithless.* Have faith in God. The

greatest good is generally done in the face of the greatest discouragements. It was a saying of Andrew Fuller, "Only let us have faith in God, and we shall not lack the means of doing good." "Lord, increase our faith," is perhaps the best prayer the disciple offered during Christ's ministry on earth.

*Hope against hope.* Nothing is too hard for God. Eliot used to say, "Prayer and pains, through faith in Jesus Christ, can accomplish any purpose." Paul said, "I can do all things through Christ which strengtheneth me."

*Let your charity abound.* Be it your meat and your drink to do good.

"Wouldst thou from sorrow find a sweet relief?
　Or is thy heart oppressed with woes untold?
Balm wouldst thou gather for corroding grief?
　Pour blessings round thee like a shower of gold.
'Tis when the rose is wrapped in many a fold,
　Close to his heart, the worm is wasting there
Its life and beauty; not when all unrolled,
　Leaf after leaf, its bosom rich and fair,
Breathes freely its perfumes throughout the ambient air."

*Be humble.* "When you have done all, acknowledge that you are nothing, that you deserve nothing, and that God has a right to do with you as seems good to him." If you attain or accomplish any thing, say, "It was not I, but the grace of God."

*Never forget the judgment-day.* Keep it always in view. Frame every action in reference to its unchanging decisions.

And now, may you be blessed of God, who " is able to make all grace abound towards you, that you always having all sufficiency in all things may abound to every good work ; being enriched in every thing to all bountifulness, which causeth," through the saints, " thanksgiving to God." Thus shall you make the most of life.

---

LOST HOURS. Lost wealth may be restored by industry, and the wreck of health regained by temperance ; but who ever again looked upon his vanished hours, or recalled his slighted years?

## SERENITY IN DANGER.

In rounding Cape Horn, a few months ago, a vessel, whose passengers and crew amounted to fifty persons, was brought into circumstances of extreme peril. An irresistible gale, which had been blowing for some days, was driving them along the shore, and at eight o'clock in the evening, the captain's computations assuring him that about three in the morning the ship would strike, and all aboard descend into the watery grave, he thought it right to inform the passengers of their danger. His own heart was heavy, too; he had beloved relatives in England, of whom he thought with emotion, while all on board was silence, and the wind continued to blow with unabated fury. "Never shall I forget the scene," he writes, " when at night Mrs. A., one of the cabin passengers, kissed her children before they were put to bed, then turning to me, with tears in her eyes, said, 'Captain, shall I ever kiss those dear children again?'" He had no words of encouragement to offer; the prospect of speedy death for all on board seemed certain; but the language of the Psalmist occurred to his mind: "Though I walk through the valley of the shadow of death, I will fear no evil; for thou art with me; thy rod and thy staff they comfort me." Entering his cabin, he sat down and wrote as follows:—

"Shall I fear when I am dying?
  Shall I shrink from death's cold tide?
Hark! an angel-voice replying,
  'Jesus Christ is at thy side.
    Evil from thy path shall flee;
    He is here to comfort thee!'

"In my heart his love I'll cherish,
  Sinking in the swelling sea;
Father, shall thy children perish,
  Who have put their trust in thee?
    No; thy Son has crossed the flood,
    And will bring them home to God.

"Still my hope, my strength shall rally,
  When I yield my farewell breath,
Through the gloom of that dim valley,
  Darkened by the shade of death.

Nothing shall my heart then fear;
Christ, my Lord, is ever near."

At about eleven o'clock, however, the gale broke; the wind shifted, and now the exertion made to avoid the shore was successful, and gratitude succeeded to fear. "Next morning," says the captain, "when I saw the lines I had written the night before, I was led to shed tears over them. I found the Lord had indeed been with me, and had answered my prayers."

---

HAPPINESS depends not so much on means and opportunities, as on the capacity of using them. And this depends so much on experience and self-control, that the probability of happiness in old age is as great, to say the least, as it is in youth.

YOUNG men, in general, little conceive how much their reputation is affected in the public view by the company they keep.

## THE CHRISTIAN SOLDIER.

A LIFE of earnest consecration to the Saviour is a precious gift to the Christian church, especially when displaying the efficiency of one devoted to the highest of all themes, and the noblest of purposes. Such a one, even under seemingly unpropitious circumstances, will exert an influence stimulating all who witness it to increased faithfulness and devotion.

Among the band of praying soldiers in the English army during the late war in the Crimea, was Captain Hedley Vicars, whose short but active career in the service of his Master was full of usefulness and promise.

For seven years after his connection with the army, though of religious parentage, he had led a life of recklessness and excess, in which from his buoyant and impulsive nature he was ever a leader. One November day, in 1851, while his regiment, the 97th, was stationed at Halifax, as he was idly turning over the leaves of a Bible, his attention was arrested by the words, "The blood of Jesus Christ his Son cleanseth us from all sin." On reading it, he exclaimed, "If this be true for me, henceforth I will live, by the grace of God, as a man should live who has been washed in the blood of Jesus Christ." After a sleepless and prayerful night he arose, saying, "The past, then, is blotted out. What I have to do is to go forward. I cannot return to the sins from which my Saviour has cleansed me with his own blood."

And he did go forward from that time with an undeviating purpose of honoring the Saviour by his life and example. The next day he bought a large Bible, and placed it open on the table of his sitting-room, and notwithstanding the surprise, opposition, and fiery persecution of his late companions in sin, declared that an *open Bible* should henceforth be "his colors." He immediately began his personal labors, which were unintermitted while he lived; and soon several of the soldiers, with some of his brother officers, were inquiring what they must do to be saved.

The name of Jesus was on his lips and in his heart, and love to him and his cause seemed the all-absorbing passion of his soul. In what he did, or said, or wrote, the engrossing object of his thoughts was apparent. His letters, even from the most interesting lands, and in the midst of the most exciting scenes, are filled with the great theme which was the burden of his thoughts. "I would willingly part with every other pleasure for life," said he, "for one hour's communion with Jesus every day."

When the war with Russia broke out, his regiment was ordered to the Crimea, where, during the trying scenes of the bitter winter of 1854–55, in the midst of toil and privation, he labored unremittingly with an intensity of interest for the undying souls about him. He denied himself every luxury and even comfort for the necessities of his poor soldiers, and though greatly fatigued by his labors in the trenches, he would, before he rested, seek the hospital-tent to talk to his "sick comrades and fellow-sinners of Jesus."

At the close of the national day of humiliation which he had desired, and which he observed with great solemnity, leading the public services with remarkable fervor, he wrote that he had derived much comfort from communion with his Saviour, and adds, "I spent the evening with Lieutenant C——. We walked together during the day, and exchanged our thoughts about Jesus." "Thus, the last word he ever wrote," says his biographer, "was the name he loved best." The next night he was with that Friend in glory, being mortally wounded while repelling a night attack of the Russians.

Thus passed from earth, at the early age of 28 years, one who ripened rapidly for heaven in a profession peculiarly exposed to temptation, and unfavorable to the growth of grace. Such a life as that of Captain Vicars, marked with such entire consecration to his Master's service, and crowned with so many precious fruits, more precious than the conqueror's laurels, strikingly illustrates the transforming grace of God, and proves to each humble follower of Christ that he too, notwithstanding the "foe within" and the "foe without," may so live as to meet death with the all-prevailing Name on his lips, and the song of victory, "I have fought a good fight, I have finished my course, I have kept the faith; henceforth there is laid up for me a crown of righteousness, which the Lord, the righteous Judge, shall give me at that day."

---

When a man is successful, people are apt to forget his difficulties, and to talk about his favorable circumstances; but circumstances are always favorable to those who can make them so.

The chief difficulty of imparting instruction often consists in awakening the wish to receive it.

## DOES THE BIBLE GROW OLD?

"What shall you do when you have read your Bible through?" asked a little child, as she looked curiously at the marks in her mother's Bible. "What will you do when you have come to the end?" "Why, begin to read it again," replied the mother. "But will you not *know* it all? When you have read other books, you put them away and read something else. Why do you read the Bible so many times?" "Because," answered the mother, "the Bible is always new; if we study it all our lives, we shall not exhaust it. It is like a rich mine of gold; you may dig and dig in it, but still the gold is not gone. Hundreds of years ago men began to dig in this Bible mine, but there is enough left for us, and for all that shall come after us. No, the Bible never grows old. So long as the world lasts, its books will be still new and living, and 'able to save to the uttermost' all who believe in them."

## THE BIBLE.

How comes it that this little volume, composed by humble men in a rude age, when art and science were but in their childhood, has exerted more influence on the human mind and on the social system than all the other books put together? Whence comes it that this Book has achieved such marvellous changes in the opinions of mankind, has banished idol-worship, has abolished infanticide, has put down polygamy and divorce, exalted the condition of woman, raised the standard of public morality, created for families that blessed thing, a Christian home, and caused its other triumphs, by causing benevolent institutions, open and expansive, to spring up as with the wand of enchantment? What sort of a book is this, that even the wind and waves of human passion obey it? What other engine of social improvement has operated so long, and yet lost none of its virtue? Since it appeared, many boasted plans of amelioration have been tried and failed; many codes of jurisprudence have arisen, and run their course, and expired. Empire after empire has been launched on the tide of time, and gone down, leaving no trace on the waters. But this Book is still going about doing good — leavening society with its holy principles, cheering the sorrowful with its consolations, strengthening the tempted, encouraging the penitent, calming the troubled spirit, and smoothing the pillow of death. Can such a book be the offspring of human genius? Does not the vastness of its effects demonstrate the excellency of the power to be of God?

---

As the relations of things often extend farther than we are aware, change may produce unexpected results; so that the longer we live, the more disposed we become to "let well alone."

## GREAT READER OF THE BIBLE.

At the late anniversary of the Vermont Sabbath School Society, a very wonderful example of Bible reading was mentioned. There is a man in that State, now ninety years old, who in fifty years read the Bible through sixty-six times. After that, in nine years and three months he read the whole Bible through eighty-six times, making the whole number of times which he has read the whole Scriptures one hundred and fifty-two. And he says he finds something new every time he reads the blessed Book. This aged Christian united with the Sabbath school when he was sixty-eight years of age, and has attended ever since.

We admire the good man's devotion to the Word of God, but we must strive to be doers of the word, as well as readers, if we would derive spiritual good from it.

## "CHRIST IN ME."

A PASTOR was pressing on his people the necessity of immediate repentance and faith in Christ for salvation. Burning words issued from his lips as he proclaimed Christ the sinner's friend, and besought all to become reconciled to him. The sermon was nearly ended. Pausing for a moment, he cast his eye anxiously over the congregation, hoping to see in some a determination to seek Christ without delay. No one, to his view, was ready to accept the offer. Saddened by the conviction, he closed the Bible, and fervently poured out his soul in prayer. "Thou knowest they *will* perish — must it be so? then give me *this* desire, 'Christ in *me*' forever." The benediction followed, and the congregation dispersed to their homes.

With a heavy heart the pastor returned to his home, entered his closet, and there before God wept out his desires. The night was a long, anxious one to that young pastor's heart. He felt that he must have his desire granted in the conversion of some precious souls.

The next morning, while seated at the breakfast table, the door-bell rung. "That is for me," said he to his wife; and rising from his seat, he met at the door an aged man, who, without waiting for a word of welcome, extended his trembling hand, and in a faltering voice said, "Sir, I have come to ask you what I shall do for my soul." The pastor led him in, and found him struggling under deep conviction of sin, needing only to be led to Christ as the sinner's ransom for guilt. Before the interview was concluded another came. It was a lady, who for many years had resisted the Spirit's strivings, and till now refused to give her heart to Christ. The pastor welcomed her in, and such a season of refreshing to his spirit followed, in leading these distressed souls to Jesus, as he had never known.

Said the lady to him, "I shall never forget your last prayer on the Sabbath. It aroused my sleeping soul. 'Christ in me.' I knew Christ was not in *me;* and if it was necessary for *you* to utter that prayer, how much more for *me*. I could not rest till I had sought the Lord Jesus." Both had been led by that simple petition to see their need of Christ, and to believe in him to the saving of the soul.

Six years have passed since that interview. The aged man has gone to his rest. Fresh in the memory of those he left behind are his dying words: "*Christ in me* — my stay, my all." The lady still adorns her profession by a consistent and devoted life. Others were led to see their lost condition out of Christ, and accept of him as their dear Redeemer. That day's labor proved to be the beginning of a precious revival, and many were brought into the kingdom of Christ. "*Christ in me*," the sinner's need, the saint's reward.

---

NOTHING but sin separates between us and God!

## SCEPTICISM.

Skepticism is the mother of credulity; the abandonment of sober, rational truth to the embrace and indulgence of unnumbered extravagant absurdities; the loosing of a frail bark from its moorings in the tempest-tried harbor of safety to the perilous dangers and storms of the billowy ocean of uncertainty, where doubt after doubt, like rolling surges, bears it far away from the light-house of reason, and passing the last lingering glimmer of eternal truth, is soon lost in the maelstrom of perdition.

---

If we could but lift the covers of men's heads, as a cook lifts the covers of the pots over the fire, to look at the contents, what a stewing and boiling we should see going on there, and what a variety of things bobbing up and down!

## INTERESTING INCIDENT;

### OR, BREAD UPON THE WATERS.

A LADY who, though an invalid, was able to converse with her friends, and who cherished a strong desire for their conversion, was sitting in her room at the close of the day, after having spent nearly all her strength in personally warning those whom she had seen to give attention to the things which make for their peace. Whilst thus endeavoring to obtain rest, a young lad entered the room. She felt as if she ought to speak to him concerning his spiritual interest. But then the thought occurred to her, "It is only a lad. He will probably have other opportunities to be warned and exhorted to flee to the Saviour." Then another thought flashed upon her mind, as though it was a voice from the spirit world, "Perhaps before we meet again he or I may be in eternity; I must address him NOW!" She immediately spoke to him, and urged upon him the importance of walking in the ways of wisdom. He listened with fixed attention; his countenance was solemn; his mind was impressed; the tears freely coursed their way down his cheeks as he hearkened to her affectionate, moving appeal. He left her and went his way. What the result would be she knew not. She had endeavored to do what she felt was her duty, and was willing to leave the result with Him who has said, " Cast thy bread upon the waters, and thou shalt find it after many days."

A number of years rolled by when, on a certain Sabbath, that lady entered a church in Providence to listen to the glorious gospel of the blessed God. Imagine, if you can, what must have been her surprise and pleasure when, as the first hymn was announced, she discovered that the preacher was that very young lad upon whom, years before, she had urged the claims of the Saviour. Her surprise and pleasure were increased at the appropriateness or coincidence of the text with what her feelings were in the last intercourse with that young man. The last words were, "Quench not the Spirit." But even this was not the last link in the chain of the interesting associations of that occasion.

The young preacher, in the illustration of his subject, referred to the manner of his own conversion, and then narrated the circumstances which have just been related, stating, that if that lady had quenched the promptings of the Spirit on that occasion, and had not spoken to him, he might still have been in "the gall of bitterness and the bonds of iniquity." Then added, "That lady I now see before me." Little did she imagine, when she entered that sanctuary, that she was going to pluck fruit from seed of her own planting, or receive consolation from one in whose heart she had instrumentally fixed arrows of conviction.

---

WAITING on God brings us to our journey's end faster than our feet.

## TO CHRISTIANS PREPARING FOR THEIR SUMMER EXCURSIONS.

A GODLY man, "whose praise is in all the churches" (the late Rev. Dr. Bedell, of Philadelphia), was alarmed to find that so many of the people of his charge returned home, after their summer excursions, without any increase of heavenly-mindedness, and having effected little or nothing for the cause of their Saviour; he therefore prepared the following, which we trust will be read and reflected upon by all those who travel *this* summer.

RULES FOR VISITORS AND TRAVELLERS.

*If residing in the country:*

1. Never neglect your accustomed private duties of reading, meditation, self-examination, and prayer.

2. Never fail to attend some place of worship on the Lord's day, unless prevented by

such circumstances as you are sure will excuse you in the eye of God.

3. Never entertain invited company on the Lord's day, and pay no visits, unless to the sick and needy as acts of benevolence.

4. Never engage in any thing, either on the Lord's, or on any secular day, which will compromise your Christian consistency.

5. Seek to do good to the souls of your family, and all others within your reach.

6. Always remember that you are to "stand before the judgment-seat of Christ."

*If travelling:*

1. Never, on any plea whatever, travel on the Lord's day.

2. Make your arrangements, if possible, to stop in some place where you can enjoy suitable religious privileges.

3. If at a public house or watering-place on the Lord's day, do not mingle with indiscriminate company; keep your own room as much as possible, and be engaged in such a

way as may make the day profitable to your soul and honorable to your God.

4. Every day, find or make time for your private duties of reading, meditation, self-examination, and prayer.

5. Carry tracts and good books with you, to read, distribute, or lend, according to circumstances.

6. Seek for opportunities to do good to the souls of those into whose society you may fall.

7. Never, by deed or conversation, appear to be ashamed of your religious profession.

8. Remember you are to " stand before the judgment-seat of Christ."

Let me entreat you to read these items of advice over and over again; and recur to them in every time of temptation. They are the affectionate warning of one who knows the danger of your situation, and whose heart's desire and prayer to God is, that you may maintain your Christian integrity, honor God, live in obedience to his will, and enjoy the peace which can alone spring from a "conscience void of offence," because "the love of God is shed abroad in the heart."

Friend reader! would it not be well to cut the above out, and paste it on the top of your trunk?

SHORT-SIGHTED POLICY. — Dr. Livingstone, in a speech at the late anniversary of the London Missionary Society, spoke of the people of a district in Africa who could nearly all read and write, the Jesuit missionaries, whose memory is still held in high respect, having taught their ancestors. He said that he would not say a word against these missionaries; but with all their worldly wisdom, they had not wit enough to give the people the Bible. If they had done so, as the Protestants had done in Madagascar, Christianity would probably have spread through the whole of the interior, and he should not have had the honor of discovering the country from which he had lately come.

## SABBATH MORNING.

Rise, my soul! the Sabbath dawns!
  Rise, and gird thee for its rest! —
While the lofty shining ones
  Round the throne, supremely blest,
Standing, wait their Maker's nod, —
Mark, my soul, the path they trod.

While they tabernacled here,
  Oft with tears their couch was wet,
Oft their hearts were faint through fear;
  Pierced with thorns their bleeding feet;
Yet to honor Jesus' name,
Gladly bore they grief and shame.

'Mid their duties and their cares,
  While their burdens made them groan,
On their path beset with snares,
  Bethlehem's Star serenely shone!
Lighting up the king's highway, —
Beaming o'er them day by day.

When their six days' work was done,
  Rested they from cares of earth;
When arose the Sabbath's sun,
  Then began their hallowed mirth;

Songs of joy and gladness borne,
Ushered in the sacred morn.

Thoughts of Christ, and how he rose,
   Victor over Death and Hell,
Vanquishing our fellest foes, —
   Thoughts of those in bliss that dwell
Free from sorrow and alloy,
Filled their hearts with holy joy.

Rise, my soul, pursue the path
   Once by Earth's redeemed ones trod,
Till these shades of gloom and wrath
   Vanish in the smile of GOD.
Rise, and with the orient sun,
Put thy beauteous garments on.

---

THE possibility of evil disturbs the anxious, but only the probability of evil disturbs the cheerful. A large part of the liabilities which hover before the eyes of the former, are never thought of by the latter.

KNOWLEDGE of the world is dearly bought at the price of moral purity.

## "TALK TO ME OF JESUS."

"Talk to me of Jesus, mother," said a little child of three years old, while lying feverish and breathing hard on his mother's lap. "Talk to me of Jesus, and let Annie get me the picture-book. There is one large and one small picture of Jesus in it." Could a parent, who loved to hear her child speak of that dear Saviour, refuse to tell the little one of what he did, and what he said; of how he lived, and how he died? His sister brought the book, and the little boy did listen earnestly to his mother as she told of Jesus, when he said, "Suffer little children to come unto me, and forbid them not, for of such is the kingdom." It was the Sabbath hour, and the mother's heart was chastened.

---

They pay too dear for fame or wealth,
Who pay in peace of mind or health.

## YOU CAN NEVER RUB IT OUT.

One pleasant afternoon a lady was sitting with her little son, a white-haired boy, five years of age. The mother was sick, and the child had left his play to stay with her, and was amusing himself in printing his name with a pencil on paper.

Suddenly his busy fingers stopped. He made a mistake, and, wetting his finger, he tried again and again to rub out the mark, as he had been accustomed to do on his slate.

"My son," said his mother, "do you know that God writes down all *you* do in a book? He writes every naughty word, every disobedient act, every time you indulge in temper, and shake your shoulders, or pout your lips; and, my boy, *you can never rub it out!*"

The little boy's face grew very red, and, in a moment, tears ran down his cheeks. His mother's eye was on him earnestly, but she said nothing more. At length he came softly to her side, threw his arms round her neck, and whispered, "Can the blood of Jesus rub it out?"

Dear children, Christ's blood *can* rub out the evil you have done, and it is the only thing in the universe that can do it. "The blood of Jesus Christ his Son cleanseth us from all sin."

REMARKABLE CONFIRMATION.—A long inscription of a thousand lines, taken from the tablets at Nineveh, was recently given to Sir Henry Rawlinson and three other eminent scholars for translation. Their translations, when compared, were found to agree, not only in the general purport of the document, but very frequently were verbally the same. The complete success of the experiment establishes the correctness of the system of interpretation by which the inscriptions on the monuments at Nineveh and Babylon have been deciphered

SLANDER no man. Remember the echo.

## FATHER, I CAN'T TELL A LIE.

Christians have been praying in Boston. A morning union prayer meeting at eight o'clock has been blessed of God, and many of the churches and Sabbath schools visited by the descent of the Holy Spirit. In one church, the Sabbath school teacher asked a little girl if she had family prayer at home. She was obliged to answer, No. She said to her father, "My teacher asked me if there was family prayer in our house, and, father, I could not tell a lie." That father was worldly-minded; but his little daughter's appeal reached his heart. He was led to serious reflection, and publicly to join himself to the people of God. He has also become a missionary of Christ to others, and his labors have already been blessed in the hopeful conversion of three or four of his former associates.

## "OUT OF THE MOUTH OF BABES."

A PHYSICIAN of high standing, an opposer of religion, was about to start for California, when his little child came to him and handed him a Testament, saying, " Pa, you must take this to read on the road." He pushed the child away in a passion, saying that he did not want to be encumbered with any such thing. His wife persuaded him to take it to please the child. On his way to the gold regions he was taken dangerously sick, and his companions were obliged to leave him, as they thought, to die. He became alarmed for his sins, and was about to give up in despair, when he thought of the Testament. He commenced reading it, and his mind was led to take hold of the promises, and to accept of Christ as his Saviour. He recovered from his sickness, went to the gold regions, and a few days since returned rich, not in the treasures of Egypt, but in that more durable substance that fadeth not away, eternal in the heavens.

---

STRIVE to obtain a heavenly frame of mind; it is worth the labor of years. Always carry a smile, and speak an encouraging word for the disconsolate. "But to do good, and to communicate, forget not; for with such sacrifices God is well pleased." Heb. xiii. 16. "As we have therefore opportunity, let us do good unto all men." Gal. vi. 10. "For of the abundance of the heart his mouth speaketh." Luke vi. 45.

To complain, is to confess weakness; and so men conceal their suffering and weariness. This makes society more agreeable, but also makes life seem to the young easier than it is.

THE relations of life are very various, and call different faculties into action; so that men are alternately leaders and led.

## RESIGNATION.

##### BY MRS. E. C. JUDSON.

Stricken, smitten, and afflicted,
    Saviour, to thy cross I cling;
Thou hast every blow directed,
    Thou alone canst healing bring.

Try me till no dross remaineth;
    And whate'er the trial be,
While thy gentle arm sustaineth,
    Closer will I cling to thee.

Cheerfully the stern rod kissing,
    I will hush each murmuring cry;
Every doubt and fear dismissing,
    Passive in thine arms will lie.

And when, through deep seas of sorrow,
    I have gained the heavenly shore,
Bliss from every wave I'll borrow,
    And for each will love thee more.

---

Trips help to save from tumbles.

## CHILD'S EVENING HYMN.

The day is gone, the night is come,
    The night for quiet rest;
And every little bird has flown
    Home to its downy nest.

The robin was the last to go;
    Upon the leafless bough
He sang his evening hymn to God,
    And he is silent now.

The bee is hushed within the hive,
    Shut is the daisy's eye,
The stars alone are peeping forth
    From out the darkened sky.

No, not the stars alone, for God
    Has heard what I have said;
His eye looks on his little child,
    Kneeling beside its bed.

He kindly hears me thank him now
    For all that he has given, —
For friends, and books, and clothes, and food,
    But most of all for Heaven, —

Where I shall go when I am dead,
   If truly I do right;
Where I shall meet all those I love,
   As angels pure and bright.

---

THE TORN TRACT. — A devoted servant of Christ in Philadelphia states that a young man strolling down to the wharf on the Sabbath, received the tract, "Warning to Sabbath-Breakers." He was so offended with its title that he immediately tore it up. Soon the thought occurred to him, "I am a Sabbath-breaker!" and he was brought under deep conviction of sin. The remainder of that Sabbath was devoted to the concerns of his soul; he was brought to trust in Christ, and to profess faith in him. He is now active in the Sabbath school, and lives a life of prayer.

THERE are many good things in this world, but it is often difficult to get them, and easy to lose them, and dangerous to use them.

## GOD DOES NOT FORGET, HE ONLY WAITS.

Rev. Dr. Taylor, of Newark, relates the following incident for the encouragement of parents to pray for their children:—

Many years ago, an old man, a devoted Christian, started a prayer meeting, which is still continued, having resulted in many and glorious fruits. As a pastor, it was my privilege to be with him, particularly during his last illness. In several visits made to his house, I found him on the Mount, looking over on to the Land of Promise. Finding nothing, seemingly, to mar his comfort or interrupt his joy, I determined to satisfy myself whether there was nothing that gave him any trouble of heart. On entering his chamber, I asked him, in simple terms, "How are you this morning?" "O, sir," said he, "I am well: why should I not be well? I am near home. Yes, I am near home — near heaven." I took the opportunity to ask him, "My dear sir, has there been nothing of late resting upon your heart, as an occasion of trouble?" He spoke not a word, but turned his head over to the wall, and lay so between five and ten minutes; then he rolled his head back upon his pillow with his face towards me, and I saw the tears streaming down his cheeks. "O, yes, sir," said he, "there is one great trouble." "What is it?" I inquired. "Speak your whole mind to me freely." "Well," said he, "I have ten children, and I have prayed to God for more than thirty years that I might see some one of them converted before I die; but he has denied me. They are all grown up, as you know, but are not yet Christians." "How do you get over that trouble?" I asked. "Ah," he replied, "I get over it as I get over all other troubles — by rolling it over upon Christ. I know that God means to answer my prayers, but he means to wait till I am gone. But he will do it; I know he will; my children will be converted."

This man has been in his grave for fifteen years, and I have watched over his children ever since his death; and now to-day I am able to say that seven out of the ten have been born into the kingdom of God, and the eighth has just experienced conversion. This is the answer to his prayer! God did not forget, he only waited; and, in like manner, he will answer the prayers of all parents who pray in faith for the conversion of their children. Let us, therefore, take courage, and lay hold upon the precious promises of God!

---

GENUINE FAITH. — The smallest degree of faith is true, is saving faith, as well as the greatest. A spark of fire is as true fire as any is in the element of fire. A drop of water is as true water as any is in the ocean. So the least grain of faith is as true faith and as saving, as the greatest faith in the world. The least bud draws sap from the root as well as the greatest bough. The least faith marries the soul to Christ.

## THE PRODIGAL'S WELCOME.

Charles was a favorite and only son in a pleasant New England home. Unfortunately, as he entered upon the excitements and pleasures of youth, he caught from infidel companions the poison of scepticism. Wealth and fashion gave to the Puritan piety of the parental heart a repulsive seriousness, and the scornful smile often betrayed the unwilling respect he rendered to the family altar. Remonstrance and tears were in vain. The hue of infidelity darkened daily upon his otherwise fine character, until at length his language assumed a bolder tone, and his disrelish of domestic religion became painfully marked.

One morning, after family prayer, he told his father, with spirited decision, that if he did not abandon the superstitious custom, he should leave home; he would go to more congenial associations, and find wealth without the annoyance of a faith he entirely rejected. His father, with grief, assured Charles that he could not demolish the altar of prayer, even if it made a final separation between them; the throne of grace was too precious to desert for a day. The sceptic curled his lip in the pride of perverted reason, and asked for his portion of money. With strange indiscretion, in too indulgent parents, it was given, with many tears and strong cries unto the Lord for reclaiming grace.

Charles went to a distant city, commenced business, formed friendships with gay and unprincipled young men, and in a year was a penniless bankrupt. In his destitution, he thought of home; and though pride struggled fiercely with conscience, and affection, he arose and started for the place of his birth. Most of the way he was compelled to walk; and on Saturday night he was within a few miles of his father's house.

He stopped at an inn, and in the morning had not means to pay his bill. The landlord opened his package, and took out a Bible.

Charles, weeping, said it was a mother's gift, and begged for the neglected volume. The landlord refused, offering to restore it when redeemed by compensation in some other form. Charles went sadly on his homeward track, lingering in distressful thought by the way, till the sun of that Sabbath was sinking behind the familiar hills. He quickened his pace, and as the full moon rose he reached the threshold of home. By a retired entrance he stole into a silent apartment. He listened, and heard the voice of prayer. Moving forward to the partially opened door, he saw the gray-haired father, surrounded by mother and sisters, bowed before the despised altar, praying for him. The rustling of Charles's agitated form drew the attention of a sister, who gazed a moment in surprise, and in a wild gush of feeling exclaimed, " O, Charles is come!" The prayer ceased, and in a moment a network of arms infolded the prodigal. The mother inquired for the Bible; a frank confession was scarcely uttered before the exclamation was renewed,

"O, Charles, we are so glad you have come!" Soon all bowed together, and angels smiled over the scene.

And is it so, that God holds an attitude as subduing to every returning sinner? When the interests of two worlds are at stake, how can the prodigal refuge to gather up his rags, and go penitently to his infinite Father?

---

AN EXAMPLE FOR BOYS. — We have a carrier connected with this office, who is between the ages of thirteen and fourteen, who occupies a seat in the highest class in our public schools, has the geography of the country at his fingers' ends, and who can cipher round a bevy of schoolmasters, and in two and a half years more, which will make him sixteen, he will probably read Cicero and Homer to boot. But in addition to acquirements at school, he has three hundred dollars in the Savings Bank, drawing five per cent. interest, and is daily adding thereto, all gathered together by selling newspapers between school hours.

## THE WAY TO BE SAVED.

WHEN convinced persons in the apostles' day cried out, What shall we do to be saved? the answer was, *Believe*, and you shall be saved. To believe in Christ, and in the remission of sin by his blood, is the first thing that convinced sinners are called to. They are not directed first to assure their souls that they are born again, and then afterwards believe; but they are first to believe that the remission of sin is tendered to them in the blood of Christ, and that by him they may be justified from all things from which they could not be justified by the law. Nor is it the duty of men to question whether they have faith or not, but actually to believe; and faith, in its operation, will evidence itself. See Acts xiii. 38, 39. Suppose, then, that you do not know that you are born of God, that you have no prevailing, refreshing evidence of it; should this hinder you? Should this discourage you from believing forgiveness, from closing with the promises, and thereby obtaining in yourselves an interest in forgiveness with God? Not at all; nay, this ought exceedingly to excite and stir you up to your duty herein. For, suppose that you are indeed *yet in the state of sin*, and are only brought under the power of light and conviction, this is the way for a translation into a state of spiritual life and grace. If you delay the exercise of faith in forgiveness until you are regenerate, you may, and probably you will, come short of both forgiveness and regeneration. Here lay your foundation, and then your building will go on. This will open the door to you, and give you an entrance into the kingdom of God. *Christ is the door.* Do not think to climb over the wall. Enter by him, or you will be kept out.

———

No man can solve the mysteries of life, but every man of common sense can perform its duties.

## THE WAYWARD SON.

A PIOUS lady had long and faithfully endeavored to lead her children in the ways of righteousness; but her eldest son gave not heed to her counsels, and with grief she saw him select a companion for life who feared not God, and establish himself in his own home *without a family altar.* But she followed him with her prayers and entreaties, and he loved and valued her, as his daily visits testified. On one occasion, as he stepped in, the title of a tract which lay upon his mother's table attracted his attention. He wished he could read it. But, no — he would not, on any account, be seen taking it up. Still, he could not leave it; for the Holy Spirit had made use of the title of that tract to arouse him from the deep lethargy in which he had so long been sunk. At last he covered the tract with his hat, drew it unperceived from the table, and left the house.

But what should he then do? He could not

well read it at home without the knowledge of his wife, and he was ashamed to read a tract in her presence. As his only resort, he betook himself to the barn, ascended the hayloft, and there devoured its pages. Deep convictions of his sinfulness followed its perusal, and he was led by its teachings to accept of offered mercy through a Saviour's merits. The mother now rejoices over her son, who "was lost and is found;" and frequently has the happiness of uniting with him *around his own family altar*, in thankful praise to their common Redeemer, and in supplications for his blessing on that Society which scatters so bounteously the leaves of salvation through the land.

---

How many a man, from love of pelf,
To stuff his coffers starves himself;
Labors, accumulates, and spares,
To lay up ruin for his heirs;
Grudges the poor their scanty dole;
Saves every thing except his soul;
And always anxious, always vexed,
Loses both this world and the next?

## HARD FEELINGS.

"Thou shalt not avenge, nor bear any grudge against the children of thy people." All those hard and unkind feelings which you entertain towards your neighbor because he has injured you, are forbidden by the Word of God, and they bring heavy guilt upon your soul. Do not try to escape by saying this is a part of the old Jewish law that has long since been abrogated. The words of the Saviour are still more forcible: "If ye forgive men their trespasses, your heavenly Father will also forgive you. But if ye forgive not men their trespasses, neither will your Father forgive your trespasses." Matt. vi. 14, 15. A more fearful denunciation against those who indulge unkind feelings towards any individual of the human race could hardly be uttered.

---

Much of " the evil of our lot " is the punishment of our misconduct.

## FORETASTES OF HEAVEN AT THE CLOSE OF LIFE.

O, THE aged, venerable saint, upon whose mild countenance is reflected the soft, holy dawn of heaven! We more than love, we reverence him. His very deadness to all the affinities of earth, makes us feel that he already belongs to a higher sphere! We linger around his arm-chair as around an oracle, and our spirits bow and worship in the sacred element of mystery which breathes around him. A thousand times blessed is the close of his life, so full of hope and immortality. The soul that can rise above the clouds of earth, can always behold the infinity of heaven, and, perhaps, every rightly taught man, before God takes him, ascends to a Pisgah of his own, from whence to look farewell to the wilderness he has passed in the leadings of Jehovah's right hand, and to catch a glimpse of the promised land, lying in the everlasting orient before him.

Christian biography is rich in examples of

such rapturous and peaceful foretastes as often characterize the closing scenes of the eminently pious. Of these, perhaps the most remarkable is that of the deeply pious and devoted John Janeway. "I am, through mercy, quite above the fears of death, and am going unto Him whom I love above life. O, that I could let you know what I now feel! O, that I could show you what I now see! O, the glory, the unspeakable glory, that I behold! My heart is full; my heart is full; Christ smiles, and I cannot choose but smile. Can you find it in your heart to stop me, who am now going to the complete and eternal enjoyment of Christ? Would you keep me from my crown? The arms of my blessed Saviour are open to embrace me; the angels stand ready to carry my soul into his bosom. O, did you but see what I see, you would all cry out with me, 'How long, dear Lord? Come, Lord Jesus, come quickly.'"

Dr. Doddridge, when near his end, said, "Such delightful and transporting views of the heavenly world, as my Father is now indulging me with, no words can express." "Light breaks in! Light breaks in! Hallelujah!" were among the dying words of the pious Blumhart of Basle. Dr. Bateman, a Christian physician, said, a little before he died, "I can hardly distinguish whether this is languor or drowsiness which has come over me; but it is a very agreeable feeling;" and, dying, he exclaimed, "What glory! the angels are waiting for me! Lord Jesus, receive my soul! Farewell!" Addison, the English poet, when near death, called a young man, who was rather indifferent to religion, to his bedside, and while he pressed his hand with tender affection, said to him, "Behold with what peace a Christian can die!"

Such language reminds me of the swan's song, which is sweetest when dying. It is like some of that language of rapture, which we find in the Scriptures, that trembled, like a thrill of heavenly joy, upon the tongues of saints ready to depart. Like that of Jacob: "I have waited for thy salvation, O Lord." Like that of Simeon: "Lord, now lettest thou thy servant depart in peace, according to thy word; for mine eyes have seen thy salvation." Like that of Paul:· "I am now ready to be offered; henceforth there is laid up for me a crown of righteousness!"

Why should not saints, "on the verge of heaven," share a foretaste of it? They have the assurance that the Comforter shall abide with them always, and why not peculiarly amid the trying scenes of death? He, as a spirit, has direct access to the spirits of saints, to fill them with his consolation and peace. Beyond doubt, also, the soul, in its last moments of stay upon the earth, is so far free from its inward affinities with the body as to see already the glorious realities of that world which it is just entering. Thus Stephen, the first Christian martyr, when his soul was about stoned out of his body, " being full of the Holy Ghost, looked up steadfastly into heaven, and saw the glory of God, and said, Behold, I see the heavens opened, and the Son of man standing on the right hand of God."

These experiences of dying saints are, of course, various in their degree; some are rapturous and ecstatic, while others are more calm and peaceful. Some have glimpses of heaven vouchsafed them while they, departing, have still sufficient strength to express their feelings; while others, as in the cases mentioned, can only yet give a faint token that joy is breaking upon them through the gloom of death. In this respect, too, there are diversities of gifts, but the same spirit. Sure it is, that in one form or other, the Comforter is doing his work at the heart.

Such a joyful, peaceful end is to be desired, not only because it tends to take away the gloom from the prospect of death, but also because of its unspeakable blessedness to the dying saint. In that hour, when flesh and heart fail, what must be the joy of such a portion! It is desirable, too, on account of those who stand in tears around our dying bed. It will take away much of the bitterness of their sorrow and bereavement to see that our death is full of peace and hope. Their farewell looks and words will lose much of their mournfulness when we see their countenances lighted up with an expression which seems to say, "I am going home!" O! the deepest of all sorrow is sorrow without hope. The sweetest of all consolation, in the hour of bereavement, is the assurance that the spirit of the departed rests — rests forever in the bosom of its God. Afterwards, too, it is the pleasantest of all the duties of love to drop the tears of affection upon the grave of one whose spirit we know to be in the Heavenly Home.

---

HEALTH is the working-man's fortune, and he ought to watch over it more than the capitalist over his largest investments. Health lightens the efforts of body and mind. It enables a man to crowd much work into a narrow space. Without it man is unfitted for the labors, the responsibilities, and the enjoyments of life.

## THE CHRISTIAN'S CROWN.

That ye may close with Christ, remember there is a sixfold crown which shall be put upon your head. Would ye have long life? Then come to Christ, and ye shall have a crown of eternal life. Would ye have glory? Then come to Christ, and ye shall have a crown of glory. Would ye have knowledge of the mysteries of God? Then come to Christ, and he shall crown you with knowledge. Would ye have eternal felicity and an uninterrupted happiness? Then come to Christ, and ye shall have an immortal crown. Would ye have holiness and sanctification? Then come to Christ, and ye shall have a crown of righteousness; yea, he shall put a royal crown upon your head, a crown of pure gold. O, what a day, think ye, it will be, when Christ shall hold your crowns in his hand, and shall put them upon those heads, never to be removed again!

## A MEDITATION.

"Who shall roll us away the stone from the door of the sepulchre?"

THE gloomy week had closed up in mysterious sadness. Dark clouds of disappointment closed down upon earthly hopes. Tragic scenes, such as were not before, such as will not be again, had transpired. Sorrowful had been the last Sabbath of the old dispensation to the loving ones whose hearts were smitten alike. It was no common sorrow. *Crucified* had been the more than brother, son, or sympathizing friend. Had he done aught amiss? No. Had he done an unkind act, or spoken an unkind word, even to his enemies? No, never. Had he not listened to every urgent call — with more than mortal tenderness healed the sick, cast out devils, raised the dead, bound up the broken heart? Did he not weep over the devoted city? Never was such unbounded benevolence, such disinterested love. Every where teaching, every where preaching salvation to the lost, pardon and peace to the penitent believing, mansions of blessedness and rest for the weary and heavy-laden.

Not one erring act, not one unimportant course, not one idle moment could be justly charged upon him. The midnight hour and mountain solitude echoed his prayers and treasured his tears. "*He went about doing good.*" Why should *he* die such a cruel death? We wonder not that his fearful, and in danger's hour, fugitive disciples were heavy of heart, and confiding woman in tears. "We trusted it had been he which should have redeemed Israel." Nor was it the Romans that had done this, but chief priests and elders of their own nation, the professed expounders of the law and the prophets, — those very doctors who heard him at first with "astonishment," and reasoned that "never man spake like this man." In process of time these same men, stung with envy, reproved by the light he shed, and by his holy life, cherished "enmity in their hearts," till they became his "betrayers and murderers."

Well might the few who followed Christ be in doubt. True, he had told them, "Behold, we go up to Jerusalem, and all things that are written by the prophets concerning the Son of man, shall be accomplished. For he shall be delivered unto the Gentiles, and shall be mocked, and spitefully entreated, and spitted on; and they shall scourge him, and put him to death; and the third day he shall rise again. And they understood none of those things." Their dark minds were not yet enlightened by the Holy Spirit. Human wisdom could not fathom such a plan as Redemption; and the crucifixion of Christ, whom they knew to be an innocent, and worthy, and lovely man, as a malefactor, by the rulers of their nation, was well calculated to bewilder their minds. They had not a distant idea of his "rising from the dead," for they had prepared sweet spices, that they might come early in the morning and anoint his body.

It was yet dark, but Mary Magdalene, and Mary the mother of James and Salome (Mark), were on their way to the sepulchre. Suddenly a new difficulty was presented to their minds. "Who shall roll us away the stone from the door of the sepulchre?" It was a *great* stone, and placed there, and sealed too, by the highest authority, to prevent the clandestine removal of the body by the followers of Christ. Did the timid, though loving ones, turn back? No. Something urged them on. They would seek out the tomb, though in doubt what would be done. Sadly strange had been the past hours. Joyfully strange were the approaching ones. "And when they looked, they saw *the stone was rolled away.*" They enter the sepulchre — but "he is risen"! — "he is not here; behold the place where they laid him"! was the message of the angel to them.

Is not here a lesson for all, and especially for distrustful Christians? Great difficulties loom up in their way. They hesitate, perhaps halt. Not so with those early disciples. Fearful, feeble, though they were, they pressed forward. ANGELS HAD ROLLED AWAY THE STONE!

---

MRS. HEMANS. — A monument to perpetuate the memory of this gifted lady has been executed in England, and will soon be conveyed to Dublin, and placed over the remains of the departed poetess. It is a small Grecian monumental tablet, in statuary, on a black ground, and is inscribed:

FELICIA HEMANS.
*Died May* 16, 1835, *aged* 41.

To which are added the following lines from her own solemn effusion, known as the *Dirge:*

> "Calm on the bosom of thy God,
>   Fair spirit, rest thee now!
> E'en while with us thy footsteps trod,
>   His seal was on thy brow.
> Dust to its narrow house beneath!
>   Soul to its place on high!
> They that have seen thy look in death,
>   No more may fear to die."

## HOW REVIVALS BEGIN.

"I WILL tell you," said a speaker in one of our Fulton Street meetings, "how the revivals began in Kalamazoo, Mich., last winter. We heard of the wonderful work of grace in this city, and in other parts of the land. We thought we ought to share in it, and not stand idly by. Still we had no such feeling as was here. We appointed a daily prayer-meeting, however. Episcopalians, Baptists, Methodists, Presbyterians, and Congregationalists all united. We appointed our first union prayer-meeting in much fear and trembling. We did not know how it would work. We did not know as any body would come. We did not know how the measure would be regarded. We came together. At our very first meeting some one put in such a request as this: 'A praying wife requests the prayers of this meeting for her unconverted husband, that he may be converted, and be made a humble disciple of the Lord Jesus.'

All at once a stout, burly man arose, and said, 'I am that man. I have a pious, praying wife, and this request must be for me. I want you to pray for me.' As soon as he sat down, in the midst of sobs and tears, another man arose, and said, 'I am that man; I have a praying wife. She prays for me. And now she asks you to pray for me. I am sure I am that man, and I want you to pray for me.'

"Three, four, or five more arose, and said, 'We want you to pray for us too.' The power of God was upon the little assembly. The Lord appeared for us, and that right early. We had hardly begun, and he was in the midst of us in great and wonderful grace. Thus the revival began. We number from four hundred to five hundred conversions."

---

HAPPY is the man that feareth always: but he that hardeneth his heart shall fall into mischief.

## EXCAVATIONS IN POMPEII.

The political state of Italy has lately taken up so much attention, that little time has been found for its antiquities. Since the discovery of the forty-seven gold coins, and more than two hundred and fifty silver coins, together with gemmed ear-rings, necklaces and collars, pearls, jewels, and costly rings, a dwelling-house has been excavated near Della Fortuna, which surpasses in richness and elegance all that has hitherto been discovered. The open vestibule is paved with mosaics, the walls decorated with tasteful paintings. The atrium opens into the tablinum and the reception-room, and the latter leads into the dining-room, which is painted with mythological subjects the size of life. Here were several trichnic couches, not unlike our modern sofas, richly ornamented with silver. The reception-room looks into a garden with a beautiful fountain adorned with numerous mosaics, and a small statue of Silenus; the basin is surrounded with the most exquisite sculptures in marble. Adjoining the dwelling is another atrium, where the servants lived. There was a four-wheeled carriage with iron wheels, and many bronze ornaments. In the kitchen, also, are many ornaments and utensils of bronze, and the traces of smoke are visible in many places, after the lapse of eighteen centuries. The apartments of the dwelling-house contained numerous elegant utensils of gold and silver, vases, candelabra, bronze coins, several cases of surgical instruments, &c. What is extremely rare, is, that there is a second and even a third story, which are ascended by a wide flight of stairs. On a small painting near the staircase, is the name and rank of the owner, in scarcely legible characters, and from which it appears that he was one of the Decurii, or senators of Pompeii. All the walls and the rooms are ornamented with comic and tragic paintings, one of which represents a young girl with a mask and a flageolet.

Hence the house has received the name of "Casa della Sonatrice," "Casa della Ercole ubbriaco." This is the most recent excavation in Pompeii.

---

A THOUGHT FOR EVERY DAY. — We see not in this life the end of human actions; their influence never dies. In ever-widening circles it reaches beyond the grave. Death removes us from this to an eternal world. Time determines what shall be our condition in that world. Every morning, when we go forth, we lay the moulding hand on our destiny, and every evening, when we have done, we have left a deathless impress upon our character. We touch not a wire, but vibrates in eternity — not a voice, but reports at the throne of God. Let youth, especially, think of these things; and let every one remember that in the world where character is in its formation state, it is a serious thing to think, to speak, to act.

## NEVER GIVE A KICK FOR A HIT.

I LEARNED a good lesson when I was a little girl, says a lady. One frosty morning I was looking out of the window into my father's barnyard, where stood many cows, oxen, and horses, waiting to drink. The cattle all stood very still and meek, till one of the cows, in attempting to turn round, happened to hit her next neighbor; whereupon the neighbor hit and kicked another. In five minutes, the whole herd were kicking each other with fury. My mother laughed, and said, "See what comes of kicking when you are hit." Just so I have seen one cross word set a whole family by the ears some frosty morning. Afterwards, if my brothers or myself were a little irritable, she would say, "Take care, my children! Remember how the fight in the barnyard began. Never return a kick for a hit, and you will save yourself and others a great deal of trouble."

## MOUNT ARARAT.

Nearly a thousand miles north-northeast of Jerusalem, in the elevated table-land of Armenia, rises this mountain, on whose side Noah's ark is supposed to have rested, after floating for a year on the waters of the flood. It lies midway between the Black and Caspian Seas, towards the south, in the region where the Turkish, Russian, and Persian dominions meet. This noble mountain is the highest point in Western Asia, and rises far into the region of perpetual snow, to the height of seventeen thousand two hundred and ten feet above the sea, fourteen hundred feet higher than Mont Blanc. Crowned with its mantle of ice and snow, it awes the traveller by its majestic grandeur, and dazzles him by its sunlit splendor. It is sometimes visible at a distance of nearly two hundred miles across a vast plain, studded with numerous villages. With deep emotion, the reader of the Bible beholds this grandest monument in the world of the judgments and the mercies of God; this second cradle of the human race, from which the family of Noah descended to people the globe anew.

Morier says of it, "Nothing can be more beautiful than its shape, more awful than its height. All the surrounding mountains sink into insignificance when compared with it. It is perfect in all its parts; no hard, rugged feature, no unnatural prominences; every thing is in harmony, and all combines to render it one of the sublimest objects in Nature."

Sir Robert Ker Porter says, "It appeared as if the highest mountains in the world had been piled together to form this one sublime immensity of earth, rocks, and snow. The icy peaks of its double head rose majestically into the clear and cloudless heavens; the sun blazed bright upon them, and the reflection sent forth a dazzling radiance equal to other suns. My eye, not able to rest for any time on the dazzling glory of its summits, wandered down the apparently interminable sides, till I could no longer trace their lines in the mists of the horizon, when an irresistible impulse immediately carrying my eye upwards, again refixed my gaze upon the awful Ararat."

The beloved Henry Martyn, in his journal of the month before he died, wrote, "On descending into the plain, my attention was arrested by the appearance of a hoary mountain opposite to us at the other end, rising so high above the rest that they sank into insignificance. It was truly sublime; and the interest it excited was not lessened when, on inquiring its name, I was told it was Agri, or Ararat. On that peak the whole church was once contained; it has now spread far and wide to the ends of the earth, but the people in the ancient vicinity of it know it no more. I fancied many a spot where Noah, perhaps, offered sacrifices; and the promise of God, 'Seed-time and harvest shall not cease,' appeared to me to be more exactly fulfilled in the agreeable plain in which it was spoken, than elsewhere. Here, upon Ararat, the blessed saint landed in a new world : so may I, safe in Christ, outride the storm of life, and land at last on one of the everlasting hills."

---

SELF-EDUCATION. — Mr. Gifford was apprenticed to the shoemaking business. He had an inextinguishable thirst for knowledge. Meeting accidentally with a treatise on algebra, having some knowledge of arithmetic, he commenced the study of the work. He had not a farthing to purchase either slate or pencil, pen or ink, or paper. Laughing at all difficulties, however, and knowing no such word as *fail*, he beat out pieces of old leather pretty smooth, and performed his algebraic operations upon them with an awl. He went on triumphantly in his career ; and ultimately became the editor of the Edinburgh Quarterly Review, one of the first publications of the age.

## DR. FRANKLIN AS A MONEY LENDER

On all occasions he was prompt to assist the necessitous, and liberal in his benefactions and deeds of charity. For public objects, his contributions were in full proportion to his means. He had a delicate way of giving money, which he called lending it for the good of mankind. To an English clergyman, a prisioner in France, whose wants he relieved by a sum of money, he wrote, —

"Some time or other you may have an opportunity of assisting, with an equal sum, a stranger who has equal need of it. Do so. By that means you will discharge any obligation you may suppose yourself under to me. Enjoin him to do the same on a like occasion. By pursuing such a practice, much good may be done with a little money. Let kind offices go round. Mankind are all of a family."

This was a common practice with him, by

which he could spare the feelings of the receiver, and practically inculcate the maxim of doing good.

---

EXTENT OF THE UNIVERSE. — It may give some idea of the extent of the universe to know the length of time required for light, which travels one hundred and ninety-two thousand miles an hour, to come from different celestial objects to this earth. From the moon, it comes in one and a quarter seconds; from the sun, in eight minutes; from Jupiter, in fifty-two minutes; Uranus, in two hours; from a star of the first magnitude, three to twelve years; from a star of the fifth magnitude, sixty-six years; from a star of the twelfth magnitude, four thousand years. Light, which left a star of the twelfth magnitude when the Israelites left Egypt, has not yet reached the earth. Our entire solar system itself travels at the rate of thirty-five thousand miles an hour among the fixed stars.

## THE BLESSEDNESS OF BEING USEFUL.

They were pious and pointed words which a Christian father addressed to his newly-married daughter: "All you can get out of life is usefulness. Some may understand the words to mean that but little happiness is to be expected in this world — that we may hope to be useful, but not be happy. If, however, any persons be useful in the world, they must be happy too. He who is useful, has more than health and strength enough to wait upon himself; he has such a superabundance, that he can wait on others too. He has more than wealth enough for his own wants, for he can spare something to relieve others' wants. He has so much intelligence and knowledge that, instead of exhausting on himself others' means of teaching, he can be himself a teacher. He has so much consolation and joy himself, that he can comfort others with the comfort wherewith he himself is comforted of God.

"But argue, if you will, that the Christian is useful, not from a superabundance of health, wealth, intelligence, and religious joy, but by self-denial and effort; I may reply that this effort is truly an effort to be happy, and implies happiness. To have our thoughts carried away from ourselves, our infirmities, our wants, our perplexities, our troubles, implies some relief. And nothing makes us feel so rich, nothing makes us truly so rich, as contriving to do some good. They are poor whose expenditure crowds hard upon their income, and who must plead the want of means when called upon to help a benevolent object. On the other hand, if persons can contrive to be useful, and to give something to promote the temporal and eternal good of others, they may best feel themselves to be rich.

"How delightful the thought that, instead of being mere helpless, burdensome invalids as to body and mind, we can think of others, can be useful to them, can help to save souls, can, on the whole, advance Christ's cause in the world, and can see, forever and ever in heaven, the blessed results of our living some years on earth, and enduring some trials there!

"It is true that there is much sin and sorrow in the world, and that we must suffer with others. But here is the very place, of all God's vast creation, to live and be useful. So far as we can understand, the most blessed angel in heaven might deem it a precious privilege to become just like some humble saint on earth, that he might directly labor in the work of doing good and saving souls.

"One of the most trying circumstances to every earnest Christian is, that he has so little opportunity of doing good; his infirmities are such, or his means are so scanty, or he has such pressing worldly cares, or the state of people around him is such as to give him little ability to benefit them. But God has given us our work to do; and we can do it, and we can be useful, and we do not know what good results will, in the end, follow from our efforts. We may do wrong to trouble ourselves about evils we cannot remedy. It may take away our cheerfulness, courage, and strength to do the good we might otherwise do. We may need to caution the young of the affliction that may await them in the world, and bid them prepare for the days of darkness, for they will be many. But faith in God is to be commended too. We may say to those who are commencing life, 'Trust in the Lord, and do good; so shalt thou dwell in the land, and verily thou shalt be fed. Delight thyself also in the Lord, and he shall give thee the desires of thy heart.' If, in brief, you would know how to be most happy in the world, study, in the light of divine truth, how to be in every way useful. Pray that you may be useful. Resolve that you will, if possible, be useful. Resolve that, though you have a feeble body and a feeble mind, though you have a scanty purse and many labors and cares, resolve that you will be useful to others besides yourself and your family, and it may have a wonderful influence in giving to every thing about you a more cheerful aspect."

## WRITE FOR EDITORS.

Their duty is trying and arduous, and their influence for good, when their heart is right towards God, is beyond the power of man to estimate; therefore, write for their paper such articles as will be for the glory of God, and for the benefit of our fellow-man. Let your articles be short, and of the best subjects. An editor has no time to dissect a long article that is of no account. Remember that Washington's and Franklin's longest speeches occupied only ten minutes.

If you have never written for the press, commence now, if the first article is but six lines. "The command is, Run, speak to this young man." If you cannot do it personally, do it through the press. You have an inexhaustible fountain to draw from; the more you draw, the more pure, if your heart is right. Make a draft from that fountain with your pen, and you will begin to see the mighty power that God has given you.

"Let us make man in our image." Hide not your talent in a napkin. God holds you responsible for your stewardship. "Exhort one another daily." Do this with your pen, through the press. This is one of the channels we have to carry the gospel to fallen man; and may every editor's heart be filled with the love of God, and may their valuable papers go to the four quarters of the globe, and preach the unsearchable riches of Christ. God is moving among us in a mysterious way. "He is doing a quick work on the earth." "What we do, we must do quickly." "He that knows his Master's will, and does it not, shall be beaten with many stripes." "He that knows to do good, and does it not, to him it is sin." Sin is among us in its worst form. Our prisons are filled with prisoners; they are manufactured at the liquor shops, and we are taxed to support them, and the liquor law is trampled upon with impunity. The only way we have to make known our wants is through the press; therefore let no talent be lost, let no paper go to the press without some article on the subjects of Religion, Temperance, and the way to prevent crime.

A friend suggests to us the following subjects for the press. Let every one contribute something. God requires it at our hands: —

First. Religion, temperance, and the way to prevent crime.

Second. Let there be a thorough organized temperance missionary enterprise. We can conquer a man by kindness, but cannot drive.

Third. Let no child be left out of the Sabbath school.

Fourth. Let parents narrate the Bible history to their children while young.

Fifth. Let a father know that his tears will reclaim a wayward son quicker than his rod. Let him take his son into a retired room, with penitent tears for his own sins, and remember God's word, " Come, let us reason together; " and " He that hath ears to hear, let him hear."

Sixth. Take extracts from Christ's Sermon on the Mount. Let this interesting part of the

Bible be searched daily, for it is the cornerstone of our salvation. If you have not time to prepare an article for the press, take extracts from this sermon, and other prominent texts that take hold of the heart, and send them to the editors; and let no paper go to the press without some Bible truth; so that the traveller, who has no Bible with him, can find in some corner of every paper he takes up a leaf from the Bible to feed his dying soul. Pin a piece of writing paper on the blank leaf of each Bible and Testament in the house, and always have a pencil with you, and when you read the Bible and find a text that takes hold of the heart and conscience, record it; and when you have no time to write for the paper, here will be a portion of the Bible always ready for the paper. Sometimes one text preaches louder than a sermon; in this way thousands will read the word of God that never attend church, or think of reading the Bible. "He that knows to do good, and does it not, to him it is sin."

"Mr. Editor, I am an executor of a will. What will you ask me to occupy four columns in your paper?" "Twenty dollars." "Was not that space occupied last week with a foolish story?" "Yes, and it cost me five dollars to set up the type." "Would it not be better for your readers to have that space occupied with fifty short pieces that have some sense?" "Undoubtedly, and they would have them, if I had the grace of God that I wish I had." "Can you not have it by asking?" "Yes, and I think I shall, when I have a convenient season." "And are you going to feed your readers with chaff while you are making up your mind?" "That is a hard question." "If you should find yourself in heaven, and Christ should present you with a crown of rejoicing, and you should see thousands there through the influence of your paper, would it not increase your happiness?" "Undoubtedly." "Are you not commanded to work in Christ's vineyard? and, as a public writer, are you not swaying the minds of thousands?" "I admit all you have said. God giving me grace, my readers shall have as good reading as can be found in any religious journal."

---

THE MOST BEAUTIFUL HAND. — Two charming women were discussing one day what it is which constitutes beauty in the hand. They differed in opinion as much as in the shape of the beautiful member whose merits they were discussing. A gentleman friend presented himself, and, by common consent, the question was referred to him. It was a delicate matter. He thought of Paris and the three goddesses. Glancing from one to the other of the beautiful white hands presented to him, — which, by the way, he had the cunning to hold for some time in his own for the purpose of examination, — he replied at last, "I give it up; the question is too hard for me. But ask the poor, and they will tell you that the most beautiful hand in the world is the hand that gives."

## EX-PRESIDENT ADAMS'S OPINION OF THE BIBLE.

Two students, after graduating from college, wrote to Mr. Adams to know what he considered the best books for them to read. His answer was, "The Bible. There you will find history, human nature, and God's revelation to man. There are many other valuable books, but let this be your principal reading. Search it daily, as for hidden treasures. When it is properly studied, it becomes the most interesting of all books; it unfolds the great mystery of godliness, and the object of this life; it prepares the heart for every day's life, and for eternal happiness with God; it will give you prudence, wisdom, and discretion in all your business transactions. My practice has been to rise early, build my own fire, take my Bible, and offer up the effectual, fervent prayer that the Holy Spirit may guide me through all truth while reading this holy Book.

In seeking God's blessing in the morning, he encamps about me through the day, and the heart is prepared for every duty. I expect to meet him in heaven, when he will unfold to me the great mystery of godliness. If you expect to sing the new song in heaven, you must follow the example of Christ."

A SISTER'S VALUE. — Have you a sister? Then love and cherish her with all that pure and holy friendship which renders a brother so worthy and noble. He who has never known a sister's kind ministration, nor felt his heart warming beneath her endearing smile and love-beaming eye, has been unfortunate indeed. It is not to be wondered at if the fountain of pure feeling flow in his bosom but sluggishly, or if the gentle emotions of his nature be lost in the sterner attributes of mankind.

GOOD resolutions may often fail, and yet grow gradually into good habits.

## DAILY DUTIES.

Happy is he who daily finds
Something to engage his mind
Worthy of his life's pursuit,
Yielding rich rewards in fruit.
Something that the mind improves,
And the part that virtue loves,
While the work, besides his fee,
*Benefits humanity!*
Oft a deed that seems but small,
Causes grateful tears to fall
From the brightening eyes of those
Who both want and sorrow know!
Often, too, a word or deed
Of kindness, in the hour of need,
Fills the widow's heart with cheer,
*And dries the orphan's briny tear!*
Actively thy course pursue,
Ever seek for something new, —
Some new work, that in the end
Clustering beauties bright will blend.
Let no opportunity
To do good be lost by thee;
Life, you know, is but a span,
*O, improve it while you can!*

Think how many need thine aid,
On the couch of sickness laid; —
Leave not thou the humble Poor
To weep, when thou canst smiles procure!
Some new act of love, each day
Performed, will render sweet life's way, —
Will heal the broken heart, and bring
*To thee a grateful offering!*
Act thy part each day, as though
It were your last one here below,
That when comes the last deep knell,
All may with your soul be well!
Thus, when life with you is o'er,
And your face is seen no more,
Your name may with the worthy stand,
A friend to Virtue and to Man.

---

A good name is not inherited from parents; it is not created by external advantages; it is no necessary appendage of birth, wealth, talents, or station, but is the result of one's own endeavors; the fruit and reward of good principles, manifested in a course of virtuous and honorable intercourse with his fellow-men.

## THE REVIVAL ADVANCING.

ALL through the month of July the interest at the Fulton Street Union Prayer Meeting has been very much on the increase. This appears in the numbers who attend, in the earnestness of prayer, in the subjects presented for prayer, and last, not least, in the spirit of humble, believing faith and confidence in God, that he will and does hear and answer prayer. It appears, too, in the willingness of Christians to labor and make unusual efforts and sacrifices to bring sinners to Christ; to use means in humble dependence upon the divine blessing. All the power belongs to God. He must convert, or there would be no conversion. Yet he works by means. This is felt and realized more and more. There is, withal, a delightful confidence in God; an inward persuasion that he hears and answers prayer speedily. We have never seen in any former revival so much of this before. And we have never witnessed such signal answers to prayer as now. Before they call, God answers, and while they are yet speaking, God hears. His people expect this, and they realize their expectations. So that in many cases they scarcely begin to pray before the blessing comes. The answers to prayer are so wonderful that God's people are themselves overwhelmed with the sublimity of the divine power in the fulfilment of his promises. The church has never seen any thing like this before. It is amazing grace! It is wonderful love and mercy! What a history could be written of the Fulton Street Prayer Meeting for the last ten months! We are now in the eleventh month of the meeting, and at no period has the interest been higher, wider, deeper than it is at this very hour. The fullest persuasion is felt that we are to see such an outpouring of God's Holy Spirit and grace as we have never seen in all the past and present, far surpassing in depth and power any thing the world has ever seen, to pervade not our city and other cities only, but our land and all lands. This heartfelt and united confidence is the *great feature* of this "great awakening." Come and pray with us, and you will feel it too. Come to the Union Prayer Meeting, and see if the conviction does not settle down deep into your soul that we are on the eve of such a revival as never yet has been witnessed. This work is all of God. He uses the instrumentality of the church to accomplish his great designs. The spirit of grace and supplication is poured upon the church — upon all who love our Lord and Saviour Jesus Christ — as never before since the church was established.

Come to the prayer meeting! you from the city, you from the country, come to the place of prayer, whether Fulton Street, John Street, or any other place of prayer, and you will *feel* all we *feel*, that the spirit of revival is advancing. This is true all over these two great cities of New York and Brooklyn. The morning meetings are fuller — also the noonday and evening meetings. Christians are crying to God. He bends down his ear and waits for their request. They are beginning to learn what the Scripture means: "Open thy mouth wide and I will fill it." The spiritual heavens are overcast. The cloud of mercy widens and deepens. There is a sound of an *abundance of rain*. Our eyes are to the heavenly hills, whence cometh our help. We have just a word to add. Let all who read this feel the importance of instant, earnest, constant prayer. Whether in city or country, in business or at leisure, pray! O, pray! Pray *for* a spirit of prayer, and pray *with* a spirit of prayer, and pray in *faith, nothing doubting*, and you shall see and feel in your own soul, that notwithstanding all God has done, we shall "see greater things than these." All you in the city come to the place of prayer; all you from the country coming into the city, come to the prayer meeting; all you who dwell in the country, have a place of united prayer, from day to day, or time to time. Let all unite to implore *such* an outpouring of the Holy Spirit as we *need.*

## ANSWERS TO PRAYER.

"A FATHER," said one of the speakers, "had three sons in distant and different parts of the country, all unconverted. He brought them to the meeting as subjects of prayer. They were prayed for as only those who believe can pray. What has been the consequence? Three letters have been received from these three sons, who have not communicated with each other, each giving an account of his own conversion." Another father requested prayer for a son at sea. He was away in the distant Pacific. His case was made the subject of earnest prayer. He has just returned to port. He was converted in mid-ocean, and just about the time he was made the subject of prayer. "I thought," said the father, "I would put down the date of that prayer meeting, and the date of that prayer. I have no reason to doubt that the prayers of God's people were answered. It is wonderful. Away at that distance God called up his attention to religion, convinced him of his guilt, led him to Christ, and the very first thing he had to tell me on landing was, what the Lord had done for his soul. He knew nothing of our prayer meetings; he did not know that he had been made the subject of special prayer, and yet the Lord has made him the subject of special grace." One of the most affecting objects of prayer was this: A father brought into one of our meetings a sealed letter to a son in South America, and laid it upon the desk, and requested the prayers of Christians that the Spirit and blessing of God might go with that letter, and make it the means of the conversion of that distant and much-beloved son. The letter was an earnest entreaty that he might become reconciled to God.

Thousands and thousands of instances, doubtless, have transpired within the last few months of wonderful and speedy answers to prayer. They are coming to our knowledge every day. "Only believe!" "Only believe!" This is the voice of God's providence, and grace, and spirit.

## UNBELIEF.

The weakness of the church is unbelief. It sadly disables Christians, and hinders the triumphs of the gospel. We are told in the Gospels of a father who brought his afflicted son to the disciples in the absence of Jesus, that they might cast out the unclean spirit which possessed him. They doubtless supposed that they could do it. But they were baffled and disappointed. Subsequently they inquired of Jesus why they had been unable to cast out the foul spirit. He replied, *"Because of your unbelief."* The same explanation may often be applied to the failures of Christians. They fail to lead holy lives. Their prayers are not answered. Their children and the impenitent around them remain unconverted. When they ask, " Why is it so ? " the answer is obvious,— " Because of your unbelief."

For instance ; it is unbelief which prevents Christians generally from realizing the infinite value of a soul, and the guilty and perishing condition of sinners. They leave it out of sight. What is the process by which we come under this form of unbelief? Often it is the product of personal sympathy, partiality for sinners. We have dealings with them, and friendly intercourse. We see their amiable qualities, and love them, as Jesus saw the young ruler, and "loved him," though he was a votary of the world. The amiable traits which they have engage our interest in them, and we stop here with a partial and sympathetic impression of their condition. We come to feel as if they were pretty good and safe, and as if they had about all that is necessary to secure for them treasure in heaven. What can Christians do rightly towards the conversion of sinners, under the influence of this superficial judgment? Can they pray for them effectually? They have lost sight of the deep and dreadful depravity and guilt of ungodly and unconverted sinners. This is unbelief, distrusting God's Word. We need to take the representations of the

Word of God on this subject, and think of them, and bring them near as realities. Then we should see that they are justly liable to destruction every moment, — that they are exposed by their own guilt to fall into hell, and that there is no reason why they are held up this moment, but the mere pleasure of a long-suffering God, whom they are provoking by their continued disobedience. "Their feet shall slide in due time." Christians need to view this truth in the light of God's Word, till unbelief vanishes. Christian, it was your own condition by nature. You were convinced of it before you attempted to flee from the wrath to come. Why should not the thought possess you, and affect you, that others are still in the same guilty and miserable condition by nature?

When Christians shake off their unbelief on this point, it is one thing which is likely to lead to the awakening of sinners; it is one means which the Holy Spirit is wont to employ to "convince the world of sin, because they believe not" on Christ.

This is one manifestation of unbelief. Another form of it, which disables Christians and weakens the church, is when they trust in their own efforts, and lose sight of their dependence on God. We must draw our encouragement, not from one another, but from God. We are too apt to be influenced to unbelief by one another. We say, "The brethren are backward and cold. The church is asleep. O, there is little encouragement." We ought to feel that our encouragement is in God. The power is his. The promise is his, that he will answer prayer. His will be the glory.

---

WHAT IS VIRTUE? — To a student, who put this question to the late Dr. Archibald Alexander, his simple and admirable reply was, "Virtue consists of doing our duty in the several relations that we sustain in respect to ourselves, to our fellow-men, and to God, as known from reason, conscience, and revelation."

## HUMILITY.

"I DWELL with him that is of a contrite and humble spirit." — *Isa.* lvii. 15.

> "The humble spirit and contrite,
> Is an abode of my delight." — *Watts.*

"Humility is not a disposition naturally existing in the human heart." — *Pike.*

"The humble spirit is that child-like, Christ-like temper, which is exclusively the effect of the almighty power of God upon the heart." — *G. Spring, D. D.*

"From a humble spirit springs all our peace." — *Young.*

"Humility, though it expose us to contempt in the world, yet it recommends us to the favor of God, qualifies us for his gracious visits, prepares us for glory, secures us from many temptations, and preserves the quiet and repose of our souls." — *Henry.*

"Before honor is humility." — *Prov.* xv. 33.

"Humility is the softening shadow before the statue of excellence." — *Tupper*.

"Richard Baxter, being reminded, on his death-bed, of the good done by his preaching and writings, replied, 'I was but a pen in the hand of God; what praise is due to a pen?'" — *Pike's Guide*.

"The greatest endowments are usually connected with the most simple and child-like humility." — *Barnes*.

"Sense shines with a double lustre when it is set in humility. An able and yet humble man is a jewel worth a kingdom." — *Penn*.

"True wisdom is attended with humility; which prepares the heart for the exercise of every Christian temper, the practice of every duty, and the honorable performance of every useful undertaking."—*Scott*.

"Blessed are the poor in spirit, for theirs is the kingdom of heaven." — *Matt.* v. 3.

"Heaven's gates are not so highly arched
As princes' palaces; they that enter there
Must go upon their knees." — *J. Webster*.

## REMEMBER THE CHILDREN.

YES, in this time of religious awakening, when the Spirit of God is moving upon all classes in the community, and so many are turning to the Lord, let not the children be forgotten. You are a parent. God has given you sons and daughters, who are exceedingly dear to you. You love them with a love which none but a parent can know. But are these dear objects of your affection Christians? Do they know the happiness of those who love the Saviour? If not, O, pray for them, and talk with them, and seek *now* to lead them into the kingdom. The present is certainly a most remarkable time, and if it passes away, leaving the children in Christian households still in their sins, when can we hope to see them numbered among the disciples? With them this should be regarded as peculiarly the accepted time.

## A FATHER'S COUNSEL.

Truth will not accommodate itself to us, my son, but we must conform ourself to truth.

Hold yourself too good to do evil.

What you can see, look at with your own eyes.

Fear no man so much as yourself.

Learn gladly of others; and whenever they talk of wisdom, honor, happiness, light, freedom, virtue, listen attentively. But do not believe at once all that you hear. Words are only words, and when they drive along so very easily and swiftly, be on your guard; for horses that draw a valuable load travel slowly.

It is easy to despise, my son, but to understand is far better.

Teach not others until you have learned yourself.

Take care of your body, but not as if it were your soul.

Meddle not with the affairs of others, but attend diligently to your own.

Flatter no man, and permit none to flatter you.

Depend on no great men.

Do what is worthy of reward, but care not to be rewarded.

Sit not with scorners, for they are the most miserable of all creatures.

Respect no canting religionists, but esteem and follow simple-hearted good men. A man who has the true fear of God in his heart, is like the sun; he gives light and heat, although he says nothing.

---

TRUE piety and devotion, ever active, and never silent, pursue their hallowed course,— "forever singing as they go," and exulting in all they possess, and in all they hope to obtain. It is not the voice of Nature which praises God, but they. It is not the hills, and the floods, and the fields which praise God, but they. It is not the land, and the promise, and the beauty, and the accomplishment of flower and fruit which praise God, but they.

## THE DAUGHTERS' LAMENT FOR THE DEATH OF THEIR MOTHER.

We are very sad and lonely, mother,
    And have been since that day
When to the cold and silent grave
    We followed you away.
We are thinking of that solemn hour,
    When, standing round your bed,
We watched your ebbing tide of life,
    As from earth your spirit fled.

When gathered round the table, mother,
    There is a vacant seat;
The smile that oft has gladdened us,
    We now have ceased to meet.
No more we hear your soothing voice
    When we're oppressed with care;
Your sympathizing love we miss;
    Our grief no more you share.

Life has lost many charms, mother,
    Since your kind spirit fled,
For we feel that our best earthly friend
    Now slumbers with the dead.
Our kindred all are dear to us,
    And we fondly love them still,
Yet there's a void within our hearts
    That none can ever fill.

When the warm, gushing tears, mother,
  Flow down our cheeks so fast,
As we call back unto our minds
  Scenes of the happy past,
And think we ne'er shall meet on earth,
  Our hearts are pierced with pain,
Although we trust our earthly loss
  Will be your heavenly gain.

The lessons you have taught us, mother,
  We'll cherish well and long;
Oft we'll recall them to our minds
  When in the thoughtless throng;
And may your spirit hover round
  Us through life's changing way,
To guide our inexperienced minds,
  Lest we should go astray.

Often in our dreams, dear mother,
  We seem to see you then;
There's a holy light around your brow,
  Such as we have never seen;
And we hear sweet strains of music,
  That thrill our souls to hear,
And in the sweetest of them all
  Your voice sounds soft and clear.

Among unnumbered millions, mother,
  We seem to see you stand;
A smile of joy lights up your face,
  As holding by the hand

The children that you lost on earth,
    That were early called away ; —
O mother! you have found them now;
    They never more will stray.

When the last summons comes, mother,
    To call your daughters home,
O, may we meet in that blessed land,
    Where partings never come!
May we meet our kindred there with joy,
    In bliss forever dwell,
Where loving friends no more will say
    That painful word — Farewell.

---

READER, would you exert a happy influence as wise and all-pervading as the influence of the press? Pray daily for editors. Pray for them in the sanctuary, in the closet. Especially pray for them *now*, when they are doing so much to determine the destiny and the character of our government for all coming time. Reader, pray for the editors of your religious and your secular paper. Pray that God would strengthen, guide, and bless them.

## POUTING JEANNIE.

Jeannie and John were brother and sister. Jeannie had a temper that was apt to fire up like a lucifer match when things didn't please her. At such times she pouted her lips until they looked as if they had been stung by a mosquito.

One day John did something which she did not like. Out flashed the angry fires from her large black eyes, as she pouted her lips until they looked twice their proper size. Her brother, who was full of good nature, laughed, and said, —

"Look out, Jeannie, or I'll take a seat up there on your lip!"

This funny remark fell like sunshine on Jeannie's heart, and changed her pouts into a smile at once. With a sly glance at her brother, she replied, —

"Then I'll laugh, and you will fall off."

Thus Johnny's soft answer turned Jeannie's

wrath into good humor. Had he pouted and spoken back, both of them would have been made unhappy. I hope the boys will all speak kindly when their sisters pout, and I hope, too, that all the girls will leave off pouting. Pouting spoils their good looks and makes them ugly in the sight of God and man.

---

IF you wish to learn music, go where it is taught. If you wish to get a knowledge of Christ, read his word, and attend the prayer meeting. Iron sharpeneth iron. If you hear a good word, be not a stony-ground hearer, but let it be stereotyped on your heart.

TEACH children to love every thing that is beautiful, and you will teach them to be useful and good.

MEN begin life hoping to do better than their predecessors, and end it rejoicing if they have done as well.

## THE SPIRIT'S TEACHING.

\* The substance of the following encouraging facts was related by a lady, who, having tasted of the bread of heaven herself, and found it to be life to her soul, lost no opportunities of offering it, in her dear Saviour's name, to every sinner who seemed perishing for want of it.

Some time since we were called by Providence to change our residence, and the day before our removal from A——, I walked round the village to say farewell to all the poor people. In my walk I met a young woman, who, in a most agitated state of mind, addressed me in these words: "O madam, I am quite a stranger here! but I know you care for the soul of a perishing sinner; my poor brother is even now dying. Alas! he knows not God; he never enters a place of worship; he is an infidel! We are living a short distance from this village; do, do come and speak to him."

Although I was much pressed for time, I

could not resist such an appeal. I accompanied the girl to a miserable abode, and followed her to the bedside of the dying sinner. His sister listened for his breathing; she raised his hand, and it fell heavily at his side. "Alas!" said she, "it is too late! he is quite insensible; I am sorry, ma'am, I have troubled you to come." "He still breathes," I replied; "nothing is too hard for God; we will speak to him; the entrance of thy word, O my God, giveth life. We will even at the eleventh hour use the Divine word; and then we will pray the Eternal Spirit to seal it upon his heart." I then slowly repeated the following texts close to the ear of the poor man: "The soul that sinneth, it shall die." Ezek. xviii. 4. "All have sinned, and come short of the glory of God." Rom. iii. 23. "Sin is the transgression of the law." 1 John iii. 4. "Whosoever shall keep the whole law, and yet offend in one point, he is guilty of all." Jas. ii. 10. "The heart is deceitful above all things, and desperately wicked." Jer. xvii. 9. "Every imagination of the thoughts of man's heart is only evil continually." Gen. vi. 5. "The thought of foolishness is sin." Prov. xxiv. 9. "Except a man be born again he cannot see the kingdom of God." John iii. 3. "Turn ye, turn ye, for why will ye die?" Ezek. xxxiii. 11.

I next began to pour in the balm for a wounded spirit. "Ho, every one that thirsteth, come ye to the waters, and he that hath no money; come ye, buy and eat; yea, come, buy wine and milk without money, and without price." Isa. lv. 1. "Come now, and let us reason together, saith the Lord: though your sins be as scarlet, they shall be as white as snow; though they be red like crimson, they shall be as wool." Isa. i. 18. "A new heart also will I give you, and a new spirit will I put within you: and I will take away the stony heart out of your flesh, and I will give you a heart of flesh." Ezek. xxxvi. 26. "For God so loved the world, that he gave his only begotten Son, that whosoever believeth in him should not perish, but have everlasting life." John iii.

16. For "the blood of Jesus Christ his Son cleanseth us from all sin." 1 John i. 7. "Look unto me, and be ye saved." Isa. xlv. 22. "Having, therefore, boldness to enter into the holiest by the blood of Jesus, let us come boldly unto the throne of grace, that we may obtain mercy, and find grace to help in time of need" Heb. x. 19; iv. 16. "For by grace are ye saved through faith; and that not of yourselves: it is the gift of God." Eph. ii. 8. "If ye then, being evil, know how to give good gifts unto your children, how much more shall your heavenly Father give the Holy Spirit to them that ask him?" Luke xi. 13. "Ask, and it shall be given you; seek, and ye shall find; knock, and it shall be opened unto you." ver. 9.

I then knelt down with the young woman, and earnestly entreated that God would water his own omnipotent Word with his own lifegiving Spirit. I then took my leave of the poor girl, begging her to come for me immediately if her brother evinced (before the morrow) any symptoms of consciousness. No messenger was sent, and the next day we left the village.

In a few years, the poor girl's sorrow and her dying brother's awful state vanished from my remembrance; but our God has said, "My word shall not return unto me void." Isa. lv. 11. About eight years after we had settled at H——, I was one day sitting in my drawing-room, when my servant said a man wished to see me. He entered the room, and with much respect and the deepest emotion, and with streaming eyes, exclaimed, " O, ma'am, how can I express my gratitude to you! I am the man whom you visited eight years since at A——. I could not move, I could not speak; but I heard every word you repeated from that belssed, blessed Book! and it pleased the God whose name is Love to make his own truth a savor of life unto life to my dead soul. I have found Jesus to be indeed ' the chiefest among ten thousand, yea, altogether lovely; and he has enabled me to hold on my way rejoicing. And I have now, after much difficulty, discovered your abode, that I might have the sweet privilege of telling you what your God has done for my soul."

Reader, do you visit the sick and the dying, and those who are dead in trespasses and sins? and are you often discouraged by your small success in entreating them to flee from the wrath to come? Are you unable sometimes to find language in which to express your desire for their salvation? Take courage from this narrative; use not your own words; seek not to conquer with your own weapons; take only the sword of the Spirit, as this lady (now in glory) did; simply repeat the very words of God, and ask of God the Spirit to seal it upon the heart, and your labor shall not be in vain in the Lord.

———————

An anxious man, expecting evil rather than hoping good, as he advances in years, is glad if he can say of life, as of a mild winter, "It is wearing away without having been uncomfortable yet."

Good resolutions may often fail, and yet grow gradually into good habits.

## PIOUS MOTHERS.

PIETY does not run in the blood, but it runs in the covenant. The following facts were gathered by The New York *Evangelist:* —

"Some years since, a hundred and twenty students, connected with the Theological Seminary at Andover, Mass., ascertained, by mutual inquiries, that more than one hundred of their number were the sons of pious mothers. Of one hundred and fourteen students, who, about the same time, were pursuing a course of study for the ministry, in connection with the Theological Seminary at Princeton, N. J., all but ten were the sons of pious mothers, and all but thirty-two of pious fathers also. In every case, where the father was a member of the church, it was also true of the mother."

Of the Union Seminary of New York, out of one hundred and twenty candidates received, one hundred and three were sons of pious parents. In eighty-five cases, both parents were pious; in sixteen the mother only.

## A MOTHER'S INFLUENCE.

IF mothers only knew the power they have over their children while young, in leading them in the way of eternal life, how different they would act. When a mother, with her little children seated around her, is instructing them in the way of Jesus, she little knows what a large audience she is preaching to; they are to go to the four winds of the earth to spread the same doctrine, the influence of which will not be known until the judgment day. You cannot commence too young; the impressions you give them then respecting the truth and promises of the Bible are seldom removed in after life. If this is omitted until they are ten or fifteen, you have then but little influence over them. Says one, "If it had not been for a pious mother, I might at this hour have been hammering stone in some prison. Instead of spending my evenings in grog-shops (as was the practice of my schoolmates), they were spent beside a pious mother, hearing the story of Joseph, Samuel, and Moses. The impressions I received respecting the Bible and the promises never could be removed in after life by any infidel shaft. Home was made attractive, and the narratives were more interesting day after day. This is the nursery of the church; if it is neglected, it weakens their powers. Learn your children to read the Bible while young. The more it is read, the more interesting it becomes. Teach them the object of this life, and the habits of industry, and economy. Teach them not to swear, lie, cheat, or steal."

"A gentleman being asked what France wants most, his answer was, Mothers." A son being brought in drunk, and laid beside his father, he asks, "Who has been giving him rum?" If his mother had taught him the way of holiness, grog-shops would have no attraction.

---

"Trust no future, howe'er pleasant;
  Let the dead past bury its dead;
Live — act in the living present,
  Heart within, and God o'erhead."

## TRAINING OF CHILDREN.

### CHILDREN SHOULD BE TRAINED WITH A CONSTANT FEAR OF OVER-INDULGENCE.

This is the one point of all on which you have the most need to be on your guard. It is natural to be tender and affectionate towards your own flesh and blood, and it is the excess of this very tenderness and affection which you have to fear. Take heed that it does not make you blind to your children's faults, and deaf to all advice about them. Take heed lest it make you overlook bad conduct, rather than have the pain of inflicting punishment and correction.

I know well that punishment and correction are disagreeable things. Nothing is more unpleasant than giving pain to those we love, and calling forth their tears. But so long as hearts are what hearts are, it is vain to suppose, as a general rule, that children can ever be brought up without correction.

*Spoiling* is a very expressive word, and sadly full of meaning. Now it is the shortest way to spoil children to let them have their own way, — to allow them to do wrong and not to punish them for it. Believe me, you must not do it, whatever pain it may cost you, unless you wish to ruin your children's souls.

You cannot say that Scripture does not speak expressly on this subject. "He that spareth his rod, hateth his son; but he that loveth him, chasteneth him betimes." Prov. xiii. 24. "Chasten thy son while there is hope, and let not thy soul spare for his crying." Prov. xix. 18. "Foolishness is bound in the heart of a child; but the rod of correction shall drive it from him." Prov. xxii. 15. "Withhold not correction from the child, for if thou beatest him with the rod he shall not die. Thou shalt beat him with the rod, and deliver his soul from hell." Prov. xxiii. 13, 14. "The rod and reproof give wisdom; but a child left to himself bringeth his mother to shame." "Correct thy son, and he shall give thee rest, yea, he shall give delight to thy soul." Prov. xxix. 15, 17.

How strong and forcible are these texts! How melancholy is the fact, that in many Christian families they seem almost unknown! Their children need reproof, but it is hardly ever given; they need correction, but it is hardly ever employed. And yet this Book of Proverbs is not obsolete and unfit for Christians. It is given by inspiration of God, and profitable. It is given for our learning, even as the Epistles to the Romans and Ephesians. Surely the believer who brings up his children without attention to its counsel, is making himself wise above that which is written, and greatly errs.

Fathers and mothers, I tell you plainly, if you never punish your children when they are in fault, you are doing them a grievous wrong. I warn you, this is the rock on which the saints of God, in every age, have only too frequently made shipwreck. I would fain persuade you to be wise in time, and keep clear of it. See it in Eli's case. His sons, Hophni and Phinehas, made themselves vile, and he restrained them not. He gave them no more than a tame and lukewarm reproof, when he ought to have rebuked them sharply. In one word, he honored his sons above God. And what was the end of these things? He lived to hear the death of both his sons in battle, and his own gray hairs were brought down with sorrow to the grave. 1 Sam. i. 2, 3.

See, too, the case of David. Who can read without pain the history of his children and their sins? — Ammon's incest; Absalom's murder and proud rebellion; Adonijah's scheming ambition; — truly these were grievous wounds for the man after God's own heart to receive from his own house. But was there no fault on his side? I fear there can be no doubt there was. I find a clew to it all in the account of Adonijah (in 1 Kings i. 6): "His father had not displeased him at any time in saying, Why hast thou done so?" There was the foundation of all the mischief. David was an over-indulgent father, — a father who let his children have their own way, — and he reaped according as he had sown.

Parents, I beseech you, for your children's sake, beware of over-indulgence. I call on you to remember, it is your first duty to consult their real interest, and not their fancies and likings; to train them, not to humor them; to profit, not merely to please.

You must not give way to every wish and caprice of your child's mind, however much you may love him; you must not let him suppose his will is to be every thing, and that he has only to desire a thing and it will be done. Do not, I pray you, make your children idols, lest God should take them away, and break your idol, just to convince you of your folly.

Learn to say "No" to your children. Show them that you are able to refuse whatever you think is not fit for them. Show them that you are ready to punish disobedience; and that when you speak of punishment, you are not only ready to threaten, but also to perform. Do not threaten too much. Threatened folks, and threatened faults, live long. Punish seldom, but really, and in good earnest; frequent and slight punishment is a wretched system indeed.

Beware of letting small faults pass unnoticed, under the idea " it is a little one." There are no little things in training children; all are important. Little weeds need plucking up as much as any. Leave them alone, and they will soon be great.

Reader, if there be any point which deserves your attention, believe me it is this one. It is one that will give you trouble I know. But if you do not take trouble with your children when they are young, they will give you trouble when they are old. Choose which you prefer.

―――――

But few nights in a year are clear enough for astronomers to make the best observations; so but a small part of life is sufficiently serene for the loftiest contemplations.

## FIFTEEN YOUNG MEN.

AT a respectable boarding house in New York, a number of years ago, were fifteen young men. Six of them uniformly appeared at the breakfast table on Sabbath morning, shaved, dressed, and prepared, as to their apparel, for attendance on public worship. They also actually attended, both forenoon and afternoon. All became highly respected and useful citizens. The other nine were ordinarily absent from the breakfast table on Sabbath morning. At noon they appeared at the dinner table, shaved and dressed in a decent manner. In the afternoon they went out, but not ordinarily to church; nor were they usually seen in the place of worship. One of them is now living, and in a reputable employment; the other eight became openly vicious. All failed in business, and are now dead. Several of them came to an untimely and awfully tragic end.

Many a man may say, as did a worthy and

opulent citizen, "The keeping of the Sabbath saved me." It will, if duly observed, save all. In the language of its author, "They shall ride upon the high places of the earth."

---

"THOU, GOD, SEEST ME."— A father and his son went out together to steal corn. When they came to the field, the father climbed up on the fence, and looked carefully around, that no eye might see him. He then began to fill his bag with the corn. "Father," said the boy, "there is one direction in which you did not look." "Ah, my son," replied the father, "and where is that?" "O father, you did not look up." The man returned home with an empty bag and a stricken conscience. There is One whose presence is more to be feared than a thousand human witnesses. There is One from whose eye the darkness hideth not. The blood and righteousness of the Lord Jesus Christ alone can cover sin in the day of his fierce anger. This is the sinner's refuge.

## THE ABSENT DAUGHTER.

FATHER S. had an absent daughter. It was a season of the special influence of the Holy Spirit, and his family had assembled for prayer. One after another of his children had been gathered to the church of Jesus; but this daughter, a gay girl of sixteen, seemed to turn a deaf ear to all warning and entreaty.

The aged father had lately felt a renewed solicitude in her welfare. His soul was stirred within him when he thought of the probability of his leaving her, the light and life of his dwelling, unprepared to meet the temptations of life or the trying scenes of death.

After much reflection, he had resolved to gather the members of his family, on this particular season, for the purpose of uniting in earnest prayer for the influence of the Spirit on her heart. It was a solemn hour to them all. The father wrestled with God until the Holy Spirit seemed indeed present with the weeping circle. Then another and another cried, with pleadings that would not be denied, for the salvation of their sister's soul.

And how was this sister, many miles away, unconscious of their prayers, spending the evening thus consecrated by them to seek her eternal welfare? Detained by a slight indisposition from the scenes of gayety she was in the habit of visiting, she had seated herself in her quiet chamber. At the very hour that her father's prayer was rising up to heaven she was reading one of his affectionate letters. The simple words, "God bless you, my child, and make you a child of Jesus," struck home like lightning to her soul.

"A child of Jesus." She would soon have no earthly father; if she could find a heavenly, how happy should she be. But how? "Pray," whispered her heart. She knelt down, but she was so bowed by the sense of her sins that for some minutes she could not speak. At last she cried, "God be merciful to me a sinner." That father's prayer of faith, and that daughter's broken cry for pardon, went up together to the throne of God.

Three or four days later a letter was handed to the father. "Who is it from?" he asked, feeling for the seal, for the old man was blind. "Abby, my dear child!" he immediately exclaimed; and opening the note with a trembling hand, called his daughter to read it to him. The first words his daughter read, were, "Dear father, *I have found the Saviour.*"

"Praise God!" exclaimed the father. "Blessed be his holy name. 'Now lettest thou thy servant depart in peace, for mine eyes have seen thy salvation.'"

As the aged man related to his brethren of the church the history of their special prayer meeting and his child's conversion, he raised his sightless eyes and clasped his hands, crying, with tremulous rapture, "Verily, the promises of the Lord are rocks that shall never be moved. Blessed be God for this glorious prophetic promise: 'It shall come to pass that before they call I will answer, and while they are yet speaking I will hear.'"

## "MOTHER IS NOT WILLING I SHOULD GO."

This remark was made in the writer's hearing, a short time since, by an intelligent, amiable youth, in reference to attending a place of worship where it is believed error is taught, and as it involves a most important principle, is worthy of a passing notice.

Obedience to parents is surely not a peculiarly prevalent principle with the young of the present day, but wherever it is seen, gives large promise of future good. Where is the young man who seeks the counsel of an experienced father, or defers to the advice of a judicious mother? Happy, indeed, were such instances common.

Parents, see to it that you exercise a watchful care over your children, especially your sons. Seek first of all their conversion to Christ, and seek it *early*, before Satan and the world have gained dominion there. Seek it in sincerity, for they will read your inmost thoughts. Daily commend them to your gracious Redeemer, and set before them a consistent, godly example, and you may expect the divine blessing on your instructions and training.

I cannot but think that the secret of so much wickedness abroad is to be found in the many irregular, ill-appointed homes of the young.

If every young man could say, "*My mother is not willing I should go*" to the club-room, to the theatre, to the gaming-table, to the many haunts of vice, and places of sinful amusement to be found on every hand, *and refrain his feet from going*, how many families would be spared untold wretchedness! how many precious souls might be rescued from eternal perdition!

---

A MAN'S tongue frequently gets him into trouble, and his friends frequently prevent him from getting out of it.

## A MOTHER'S PRAYER ANSWERED.

In one of the late meetings in Fulton Street church, New York, a gentleman requested prayer for a brother-in-law. He was, he said, in this room for the first time at a prayer meeting last night. He is here in this business men's prayer meeting for the first time to-day. The Spirit of God met him here last night. He came here as thoughtless as ever — just returned to the city from Newport, where he had spent the summer. This morning, before he left his room, I was sent for to come and converse with him and pray for him. I found him in great anguish of mind, on his knees, in a flood of tears, engaged in prayer, in broken sentences calling on God for mercy. Now I want you to pray that this may be the hour of his deliverance, — that he may be converted now and here, — find to-day pardon and peace in believing in Jesus. I will just add, this man had a very pious mother, who died when he was thirteen years of age. Often, he says, has he felt the tears of his mother raining down on his hands, as she knelt beside him and over him in prayer. Twenty-five years ago that devoted mother went to her rest in the heavens. But all her prayers and tears seem to have had an instantaneous resurrection in the mind and heart of her son, and here and now, it may be, that God designs to answer that mother's prayers.

Two days afterwards this same man, for himself and of his own accord, put before the Fulton Street meeting a request that they would unite with him in thanks to God, who hears prayer, for the hope he had that his sins had been forgiven, and that he had been converted from the error of his ways, and made a new creature in Christ Jesus, begging a continued interest in their prayers, that his faith and confidence in the Saviour may be strengthened.

## THE MOTHER'S FAITH. — A FACT.

"I should like to know what mother thinks of the Lord now!" exclaimed a little boy of ten years, as a group of half-starved brothers and sisters were preparing for school, without a breakfast, one bitter cold morning.

Well knew each member of that hungry band of little ones, that through all the trying scenes of poverty in their father's long illness, a firm and unwavering faith had upheld their praying mother. But now, when the last fire had been made, and the last frugal meal of baked potatoes eaten, and her own frail form was sinking beneath its burden of work and sorrow, the climax seemed reached. "What does mother think of the Lord now!" fell upon the ears of one of the loveliest women I ever met. It was from the lips of her first-born, for whose submission to God she had ever been hoping and striving. The words fell upon her heart like lead. It was a new test of her sorely tried faith, a new drop added to her bitter cup.

A long and severe sickness of her husband had reduced them to extreme poverty, and with no resource but the needle, it had been difficult to meet the demands of a large family and perform sick duties at the same time. When this eventful morning dawned, there was no more food in the house, and just wood enough to build one more fire. A slice of borrowed bread was toasted for the sick man, and his pillowed chair drawn before the last fire. He knew not the destitution, the toil, the self-sacrifices that oppressed his wife; he saw only the smiles, the industry, the neatness, and the patient waiting for brighter days.

When the daring words of the hungry boy fell upon that Christian mother's ear, she just lifted up her heart in the silent eloquence and fervor of ejaculatory prayer, known only to the toil-worn and working disciple. The answer came, "The Lord is good; his mercy endureth forever." Her heart responded, and as she raised her eyes to the window, two good loads of wood standing there testified that she had not thought too much of her heavenly Father, or trusted to his promises too long. The sun shone again on that household, and never more did Henry say, "I wonder what mother thinks of the Lord now!"

---

BREAK up your fallow ground, and cultivate it with heavenly thoughts, and then there will be no room for vain or vicious thoughts.

COMMIT to memory Christ's Sermon on the Mount, and preach it from house to house.

"DID not our heart burn within us while he talked with us by the way, and while he opened to us the Scriptures?"

"WATCH ye here, while I go yonder and pray."

"CAN ye not watch one hour?"

## REV. WARREN BURTON'S QUESTIONS.

1. At how early an age should a child be made to obey?
2. Must a reason always be given for a requirement?
3. Is it well to secure obedience by the promise of some indulgence?
4. What is the consequence of promises or threats by parents, being left unfulfilled?
5. What is the consequence of yielding to a child's teasing?
6. What will be the consequence of artifice with a child?
7. How can parental authority best be maintained?
8. What differences must be made with different dispositions?
9. Is it necessary for children ever to get beyond the control of their mothers?
10. How can parents best retain the confidence of their children, consistently with due authority?

11. What motives should be addressed to the young?

12. How are children to be induced to act from right motives?

13. How shall a child be trained to self-government?

14. What is the best way to foster a spirit of self-sacrifice?

15. Can any favoritism, among their children, be properly manifested by parents?

16. What are the effects of disagreement between the father and the mother respecting modes of managing the children?

17. If such disagreement cannot be avoided, ought it to be expressed in the presence of the children?

18. What effect have luxuries for the palate on the health of children?

19. What is the effect of much of the light reading of the present day on the character of the young?

20. How shall a benevolent disposition and a love of doing good be cultivated?

21. Ought young children to be encouraged to give to charitable objects?

22. What is the influence of incidental and apparently trivial circumstances on the character of a child?

23. Can we separate between education for this life and education for the life to come?

24. What is the influence of reading the Bible, and of family prayer, on children?

25. What importance may be attached to the praying of a parent alone with a child, on occasion of any uncommon delinquency or sin?

26. What is the importance of prayer alone with a child, occasionally, without any special call from immoral occurrence, but simply as a matter of religious training?

27. At how early an age, and in what manner, should the first religious impressions be made?

## REGENERATION.

#### WRITTEN BY A LITTLE GIRL.

By the term Regeneration, a new birth is meant, — that work of the Holy Spirit which we experience, through the ordinances of the church, by faith in the Saviour, — a change of heart. It does not signify merely a reformation of the outward conduct, so that we appear to do that which is right in the sight of men, but it is a complete change of the whole person. It is such a union of man with his Creator, that he is enabled by it to perceive the true excellence of every thing he has made, because he sees every thing related to his glory. It is spoken of in the Holy Scriptures as a New Birth, born from Heaven. It implies a partaking of the divine nature, in the person of Jesus Christ, by which we become released from sin, and rendered capable of enjoying spiritual and refined pleasure. The efficient cause of regeneration is the divine Spirit. That man himself is not the author of it, is evident, if we consider the state in which he is, before it takes place. It is a state of complete ignorance, and utter inability to do any good thing. A true knowledge of the nature of the work to be done in regeneration, will enable us to perceive plainly that it is not in the power of man to perform it. It is termed a New Creation, alluding to the creation of the natural universe; a new life, a new being, formed out of elements which before had no existence properly for man. Besides, it is expressly denied to be of man, and affirmed to be of God: "Which were born not of blood, nor of the will of the flesh, nor of the will of man, but of God." It is the work of God's Spirit, blowing where it listeth, the sound of which we hear, but cannot tell whence it cometh or whither it goeth; even so is every one that is born of God.

The evidences for which we should look, that such a change has been produced within us, are, sorrow for sin, repentance towards God, faith in Jesus Christ, and the presence of a love to God which creates a constant and joyful obedience to his precepts and commandments, — a willingness to spend and be spent in promoting his glory and the spiritual interest of man. These evidences make it quite clear to the world, as well as to his own mind, that he is the subject of this great change; and with a humble confidence, in which the certitude is greater because of its humility, directing his eye towards his spiritual home, he can say, " My Father, who art in heaven."

> "My Father, God! how sweet the sound!
> How tender, and how dear!
> Not all the harmony of heaven
> Could so delight the ear."

---

YOUR time is your money. Spend none of your precious golden moments over that which is worthless. Give your time a commercial value.

## A SMILE AND A TEAR.

Two sisters met in fairy land,
And took each other by the hand;
   Their names were Smile and Tear.
Smile, looking up with sparkling eye,
Espied the earth just rolling by,
   And said, "Let's wander there.

"We'll go and make it very glad;
Come, sister Tear, don't look so sad;
   Can you no joy impart?"
"Ah, sister Smile," the Tear replied,
"You little know the joy I hide,
   When gushing from the heart."

At length, with sad and pitying eye,
Tear bade her fairy land good by,
   And so they took their flight.
They reached the earth at dawn of day,
And wandering through a forest gray,
   A cottage came in sight.

A lady at the window sat;
Tear quickly dropped into her lap, —
   For one was yet away;

The sparkling bowl all night filled high,
He drank, and drained the dregs till dry, —
    How long did seem his stay!

Her infant gazed into her eye,
Then drew a long and deepened sigh,
    As if her grief to trace;
The mother kissed its little cheek, —
How pure, how innocent, and meek
    The smile which lit its face!

A laughing cherub, rosy boy,
Came bouncing in, all full of joy, —
    "O mother, father's come!
He's signed the pledge, the medal's here,
He'll drink no longer rum or beer,
    But stay with us at home!"

That day the cottage hearth was glad,
For rum no longer made it sad, —
    The pledge had sealed it down!
Smile tried in vain to play her part,
Tear took possession of each heart, —
    Thrice happy was that home!

A widow ate her scanty fare,
All lonely, then breathed out a prayer, —
    The fierce winds whistled by;

No cheerful fire was in her grate,
Yet she toiled on, all cold, till late, —
   No tear was in her eye!

Bright morning came with frozen air,
But God had heard the widow's prayer;
   A friendly hand was near
Who knew her wants, supplied them well;
The widow's joy Smile could not tell, —
   It gushed in every tear!

A maiden by the sea-side lone,
Sat watching for a lover gone;
   A little speck she spies, —
A sail, — he comes, — it nears, it nears!
How poor are smiles, how rich are tears,
   To test such truthful ties!

Smile turned aside: "Ah, sister Tear,
This world for me is far too drear,
   It loves you much the best.
I only play upon the face,
And dazzle for a little space,
   You dwell within the breast!"

The sisters now each took their flight:
Smile quickly soared up out of sight;
   Tear felt 'twas hard to part, —

> Poised on her wing, she gazed behind,
> Then threw her mantle on mankind,
> To cheer the broken heart!

---

THE UNBLESSED MEAL.—Thirty years ago a little boy, the son of pious parents, was invited to spend a few days at the house of a friendly family. When dinner came on the table, Philip, very hungry after his journey, could not be persuaded to touch a morsel of food. Again and again did they urge him to eat, and as often did he look wistfully at the contents of the table, but resolutely declined. At length the lady kindly inquired if there was any reason why he could not eat his dinner. Bursting into tears so that he could scarcely speak, he exclaimed "You haven't blessed it!" That family ever afterwards asked the blessing of God on their food, and that little boy is now a missionary in Jamaica.

## EVENING HYMN OF A GOOD BOY.

How sweet to lay my wearied head
Upon my quiet little bed,
And feel assured, that all day long,
I have not knowingly done wrong.

How sweet to hear my mother say,
"You have been very good to-day;"
How sweet to see my father's joy,
When he can say, "My dear good boy."

How sweet it is my thoughts to send
To many a dear-loved distant friend,
And think, if they my heart could see,
How very happy they would be.

How sweet to think that He whose love
Made all the shining world above,
My pure and happy heart can see,
And loves a little boy like me.

---

NEVER go to a theatre. The prayer meeting is far better.

## THE GOOD SHEPHERD.

At one of our pleasant social evening meetings, our pastor took for the subject of familiar remark that beautiful Psalm, the twenty-third, "The Lord is my shepherd, I shall not want." He enabled us to feel how pleasant, how delightful, how blessed it was to have Jesus our Redeemer for our shepherd. The green pastures, the still waters, were all before us, and especially how cheering it was, to know that such a one as our shepherd would indeed pass with us through the "dark valley and shadow of death." Just then, I can hardly say why, my eye turned almost involuntarily to two persons who sat at some distance from me; and a little colloquy, which I had somewhere read, flashed upon me. Possibly the thought of it might have turned my attention to them, or else my glance at them might have suggested it — the which I cannot say. The young couple were dressed in deep mourning; they had just laid away a dear little babe in the grave. The colloquy was as follows, and it came to me as part and parcel of the reflections of the hour: "And what does the shepherd do when one of the flock does not follow?" "O, he takes up the little lamb, and then the mother will follow readily enough." I thought how many beautiful, darling children Jesus had taken away this year, and I said "May not this be one way which he is taking, to rouse his sleeping, dilatory servants?" My inference *was not* that such were faulty above others. O, no, that is not the Bible rule of judging. "Whom the Lord *loveth* he chasteneth;" but in this time of general deep declension something is necessary; and may we not hope that these afflicted ones which, throughout our borders are even so many, shall exercise an enlivening influence in every several flock where they may be found? So we trust, so we believe. It is in Affliction's darkest hour that the most precious, heavenly light breaks forth upon the soul. How kind is Jesus in that hour! He, as it were, weeps with us, as at the grave of Lazarus. But he will not have us yield ourselves up to tears. Are there any, who, under circumstances like those alluded to above, are sitting down, disconsolate and inactive in their grief? That is not the way. The following anecdote, to me, is interesting, perhaps it may be of use to others. It was related to me, in substance, by an elderly lady, who, after a long walk to church, used occasionally to spend the summer intermissions at noon at our house: —

Many years ago, when comparatively in her youthful days, that Christian woman had a beautiful child. It was very different, she said, from other children. It had a seriousness of aspect, a thoughtfulness, when a mere babe in the arms, unusual and unexpected. It took in the thoughts of God, of heaven, of dying, with its first lisping efforts. The mother thought the child heaven-born — she knew not when. Meanwhile the frail casket restraining the infant immortal was crackling and break-

ing, and the young spirit flew away *so gently*
— but it was gone, to know earth's taint and
stain no more. The mother grieved and wept
exceedingly. She knew that God had done it —
it was right; but how to stop that heartache.
By night and by day it was all the same.
One night she dreamed: she was wandering;
she had lost her child. A weary way she had
traversed, when suddenly, to her inexpressible
joy, she found it! She clasped it in her arms,
she ran with all haste to her dwelling. She is
about to enter with her long-lost, now recovered, child. Just at the threshold of her door
stands her Lord and Saviour. She recognizes
him. He looks upon her with something of
a smile and a rebuke, puts forth his hand and
takes the child, saying, "It is mine now."
The mother woke. She wept no more. "God
speaketh once, yea twice, yet man perceiveth it
not. In a dream, in a vision of the night, when
deep sleep falleth upon men, in slumberings
upon the bed. Then he openeth the ears of
men, and sealeth their instruction."

## YOUNG MEN.

There is no moral object so beautiful to me as a conscientious young man. I watch him as I do a star in heaven; clouds may be before him, but we know that his light is behind them, and will beam again; the blaze of others' popularity may outshine him, but we know that, though unseen, he illuminates his own true sphere. He resists temptation, not without a struggle, for that is not virtue, but he does resist, and conquers; he bears the sarcasm of the profligate, and it stings him, for that is a trait of virtue, but heals with his own pure touch. He heeds not the watchword of Fashion, if it leads to sin; the atheist, who says not only in his heart, but with his lips, "There is no God!" controls him not; he sees the hand of a creating God, and rejoices in it.

Woman is sheltered by fond arms and loving counsel; old age is protected by its experience, and manhood by its strength; but the young man stands amid the temptation of the world like a balancing power. Happy he who seeks and gains the prop and shelter of religion.

Onward, then, conscientious youth! Raise thy standard, and nerve thyself for goodness. If God has given thee intellectual power, awake in that cause; never let it be said of thee, he helped to swell the tide of sin by pouring his influence into its channels. If thou art feeble in mental strength, throw not that drop into a polluted current. Awake, arise, young man! assume that beautiful garb of virtue! It is difficult to be pure and holy. Put on thy strength, then. Let truth be the lady of thy love — defend her.

---

YOUR character cannot be seriously harmed, except by your own acts. If any one speaks evil of you, let your life be so that none will believe him.

## A SERMON REMEMBERED EIGHTY-FIVE YEARS.

Luke Short, when about fifteen years of age, heard a sermon from the celebrated Flavel, and soon after went to America, where he spent the remainder of his life. He received no immediate impression from Flavel's sermon, and lived in carelessness and sin till he was a century in age. He was now a " sinner a hundred years old," and to all appearance ready to " die accursed." But, sitting one day in a field, he fell into a busy reflection on his past life; and recurring to the events of his youth, he thought of having heard Mr. Flavel preach, and vividly recollected a large portion of his sermon, and the extraordinary earnestness with which it was delivered. Starting, as if stung by an adder, he instantly labored under accusings of conscience, and ran from thought to thought till he arrived first at conviction of sin, and next at an apprehension of the divine method of saving the guilty. He soon after joined a Congregational church in his vicinity, and to the day of his death, which happened in the *one hundred and sixteenth* year of his age, gave satisfactory evidence of being a truly converted and believing follower of the Saviour. Mr. Flavel had long before passed to his heavenly rest, and could not, while on earth, have supposed that his living voice would so long continue to yield its echoes as an instrument of doing good to a wandering sinner. Let ministers and private Christians, who labor for the spiritual well-being of their fellow-men, cast their bread upon the waters, in full faith, that though they lose sight of it themselves, it shall be found after many days.

---

The best capital for young men to start with in life, is industry, good sense, courage, and the fear of God. It is better than all the friends or cash that was ever raised.

## HOW TO MAKE HOME ATTRACTIVE.

If parents knew the power they have over their children, while young, to make home attractive, and the influence it would have over them in after life for their good, they would spare no pains in this direction. Always treat them with a smile; reprove them gently; narrate to them, from day to day, the interesting facts of the Bible, and the manner in which they follow its teachings will be an index to their happiness here and hereafter. When properly studied, it becomes the most interesting of all books. Learn them habits of industry and economy while young. This will draw their attention away from places of amusement, which have a tendency to pride, vanity, and sin. Take an interest in the reading you select for them; sympathize with them in all their affliction, and they will soon learn that there is no place like home.

## DOMESTIC EDUCATION.

### BY REV. H. WINSLOW.

WHAT a charm pervades that dwelling, whose matron has the grace of a thorough domestic education! An air of neatness, order, simplicity, cheerfulness, pervades and blesses all. The very atmosphere is sweet. You scarcely enter the door before unequivocal signals betoken the presiding angel within. The door-stone is so clean, the door-handle so bright, the mat, hat-stand, and other entry conveniences so tidy and befitting, the air so pure, the servant, in neat apparel, and with smiling face, opens the door so generously, that the first impression is, *Here is home, sweet home.*

Nor does a further ingress and more close observation disappoint you. If costly drapery does not hang at the windows, nor princely carpets grace the floors, nor sparkling chandeliers and dazzling ornaments display their owner s wealth, — things not unfrequently serving only as miserable apologies for the truer ornaments, — every thing around you bears record that the eye of taste and the hand of diligence have been freshly upon it. How bright the steel and brass; how clean the hearth; how luminous the windows; how free from dust the sofas, chairs, and every thing around you! The entire room has an air of purity, comfort, and hospitality. How easy and tasteful the arrangements. That book-case, with its well-chosen volumes; that centre-table, with its choice specimens of thought and skill; the vase in yonder corner, displaying the beauties of a well-cleansed and watered green plant, unfolding its luxuriant leaves and opening its bright-eyed blossoms, as if to smile gratitude on its worthy benefactress, — all evince this the home of one who knows how to live, and make home happy.

One fear is well-nigh apprehending you; you can hardly touch but to soil, and your presence is thus tempted to question its welcome. But that fear is banished the moment the lady enters. That cordial and generous smile, that charming benevolence which only a true heart can yield, and which all true hearts can appreciate, puts you instantly at ease, and makes you regardless of all but objects of mutual and real interest. It is no longer the house, the room, the furniture; it is that, only that, for which you are present, whether it be a call of business, charity, or friendship.

But the parlor is, perhaps, not the best place to furnish decisive tests of the highest order of domestic education. There are, at least, four places more unequivocal — the kitchen, the cellar, the store-closet, and wardrobe. Well, let us take a look at these; for though the good lady has no vanity to gratify, she has the benevolence to gratify our reasonable curiosity, and she is entitled to an honest confidence that she has nothing to fear from our eyes.

The kitchen is, if possible, more attractive than the parlor. It is only an hour since breakfast, and yet every thing is cleaned and restored to its place. The floor, the sink, the tables, and all the kitchen appurtenances, are so pure, sweet, and wholesome, that health and comfort seem there to have found their most favored home. I would as soon take a lunch there as in the king's dining-room. I half think it would taste even better, especially if ministered by the lady's own hands.

Shall we enter the cellar? Here, too, the same neatness, order, convenience, and economy are every where seen. The barrels are arranged in order against the wall; the floor is cleanly swept; no cobwebs impend from the ceiling or beams above, and the purity of the air proves at once the cleanliness and careful ventilation of this subterranean department. On that stand are the brushes, and the conveniences for cleaning and polishing shoes; here is the well-arranged vegetable and provisionary department; there, perhaps, the wash-tubs and benches; — in a word, nothing is in this cellar which ought not to be here and every thing which ought to be here is here, and in the right condition. Such is a good housewife's cellar. Even the impudent rats themselves, and the more lawless mice, seem to have learned that this is holy ground; their impious feet never defile it.

We may be indulged a look into the store-closet. Here, again, we find the same order, neatness, economy. The coffee, teas, sugars, spices, &c., are all neatly arranged and well covered; the less bulky articles are placed in small, tight boxes, each carefully labelled; the preserves are carefully kept from becoming acid or mouldy by close covering, cool position, and occasional scalding; the fruits are inspected, sorted, and used with a promptness that forestalls decay and waste; the cheese is kept in a tight, cool vessel, and the cake is also carefully stored in stone or earthen, to keep it fresh and sweet; in a word, all things here evince that the guardian spirit of this house knows the secret of true comfort with true economy.

Perhaps we ought not to intrude into the wardrobe; and, indeed, after what we have seen, it may appear needless to do so. But there are two or three things here which we cannot forbear to notice. The first is the order with which the articles are arranged. Each member of the family has his place. His clothes are hung, or laid in drawers, and a place exclusively assigned to him; so that the mother, the servant, or even the child, could get any article wanted in the dark. This saves all waste of time and temper in search of mislaid clothing. The next thing to be noticed is the carefully preserved integrity of each article. Nothing is placed here but in a condition to be worn;—not a hole or rent in a single article,—so that all of this family are saved the vexatious liability of being obliged to dress over a second or third time to secure a sound garment. Another thing to be noticed is the cleanliness of the articles, the whiteness of the linens, and the entire absence of every thing that could betoken the presence of a moth. After what we have seen, we may safely conclude that all is right in this house. If peace, content, abundance, a happy husband and virtuous children, are not found here, it is not, we presume, the fault of the wife. Something more, however, remains to be said on this subject.

VALUE OF TRACT OPERATIONS. — A colporter in Michigan, says the Messenger, who has explored a large portion of twelve counties, containing an area of seven thousand nine hundred and seventy-seven square miles, says, " I find that wherever the Society's publications have been circulated, a salutary influence has been exerted. Churches have been formed and strengthened. Houses of worship have been erected. Sabbath schools have been organized. Children have been brought under the influence of pious example and instruction."

YOUNG men, in general, little conceive how much their reputation is affected in the public view by the company they keep.

## THE SINGING STUDENT BOY.

Many years ago a student boy was seen and heard in the streets of an ancient town singing. He was a stout, plainly-dressed boy, but his face was pale, and his eyes were sad and tearful. His voice was most musical, and the songs he sang were in beautiful words and about sacred things. Every time he finished a song he stepped to the door of a house and gave a gentle tap. When it was opened, he said, in gentle tones, —

"Please give a poor student boy a morsel of bread."

"Begone with thee, thou beggar child!" was the rough reply that met his ear as the poor child shrank from the door-steps.

Thus driven from door to door, he sang his sweet songs until his body was weary and his heart sad. Scarcely able to stand, he at last turned his steps homeward. Striking his noble forehead with his hand, he said, —

"I must go home to my father's house, and be content to live by the sweat of my brow. Providence has no loftier destiny for me. I have trodden out its paths by aiming higher."

Just at that moment Ursula Cotta, a burgher's wife, who had heard his songs, and seen him driven from a neighbor's door, felt her heart yearn with pity towards the helpless boy. She opened her door, beckoned to the young singer, smiled sweetly upon him, and in tones that sounded like heavenly melodies to his ears, said, —

"Come in, poor boy, and refresh thyself at my table."

Happy little singer! How he enjoyed the delicious meal! And when the good dame and her husband told him to make their house his future home, his heart melted. With eyes half blinded with tears, he looked in the face of his friends, and said, —

"I shall now pursue my studies without being obliged to beg my bread from grudging hands. I shall have you, sir, for a father, and you, sweet Ursula, for a mother. My heart will once more learn to love. I shall be happier than I can express."

After that day the singing boy studied hard and well. Years afterwards the world heard of him, for it was he who uttered his voice against Popery, and became the chief of that Reformation which gave an open Bible to the world. His name was MARTIN LUTHER.

Courage, then, poor boy! You may be friendless and unknown to-day — you may have to plod through trials and toils, uncheered by the smiles of even a sweet Ursula. But never mind. Plod away. Stick to study and duty. God cares for you. He has a work for you to do, and if you are faithful and true, he will, in due season, put you in your proper place. Toil on.

---

TO-MORROW never comes. Live to-day as if it were your last day to live, — soberly, faithfully, diligently, cheerfully, and prayerfully.

## THE PRICE OF A BLESSING, AND THE MEANS OF OBTAINING IT.

In the first place, have perfect, childlike faith in Christ, and what God has said respecting him. Without faith it is impossible to please God. In the second place, address the Father through Christ. "Whatsoever you ask the Father in my name, that he will give it you." In the third place, carry no worldly thoughts to the throne of grace; remember that is holy ground. Moses was commanded to take off his shoes. Carry nothing but Christ and the object of your petition. We trust you have asked God to forgive all your sins, and those of your enemies, and you have forgiven them yourself. "If you do not forgive men their trespasses, neither will your heavenly Father forgive you." This is the price of a blessing.

You may be afflicted, you have lost all of your children but one, and that is sick. Your doctor has called, and can give you no hope.

Your heart is full. You think of one more Physician you have not consulted. You have resolved to seek his blessing. You are on your way to your retired room. You bathe your footsteps with penitent tears. You find yourself in your retired room; the door is closed. You hear a voice saying, "According to your faith be it done unto you." You prostrate yourself at the feet of Jesus, and bathe them with your tears. "Father, if it be possible, let this cup pass from me; nevertheless, not my will, but thine be done, in the name of the Lord Jesus Christ. Amen." You hear a knock at the door; your doctor has called to inform you that your child is recovering. Yes, the message has gone forth, and echoed back, "Your child shall live!" and it does live. Your faith has saved your child.

Take the example of the Indian woman. After losing all her children but one, and that sick, she goes out doors, and throws up her arms, and says, "O thou Everywhere, have mercy on my child!" The message echoed back, "Your child shall live!" and it did live. This is the power of faith. "According to your faith, be it done unto you." If you go to the throne of grace, and do not obtain a blessing, be not discouraged. It may be God is trying your faith, or you have some sin that has not been forgiven. Go often. Christ has set you the example. He went away three times, saying the words, "Father, if it be possible, let this cup pass from me; nevertheless, not my will, but thine be done."

---

COMMON PATHS. — It sometimes seems to us a poor thing to walk in these common paths wherein all are walking. Yet these common paths are the paths in which blessings travel; they are the ways in which God is met. Welcoming and fulfilling the lowest duties which meet us there, we shall often be surprised to find that we have unawares been welcoming and entertaining angels.

## AN ENCOURAGING WORD FOR THE PHILANTHROPIST.

A GENTLEMAN seeing a sick lady drinking at a fountain, asked her if she had drank at the great Fountain. She soon after informed him she had drank at the great Fountain, and was healed, and was soon to drink of it in the kingdom of heaven.

A gentleman meeting a young man resting his oxen, spoke to him of Christ. It was the means of his conversion.

A gentleman meeting a friend, and learning his parents had not found Christ, engaged to remember them at the throne of grace. He was soon informed that his prayers were answered.

A stranger said, "The book you handed me was the means of making a man of me. I was a wild, crazy-headed youth. I have been one voyage to sea, and returned home, and united with the church."

A gentleman meeting a friend with these words, "What think ye of Christ?" It was the means of his conversion.

A gentleman, rising in prayer meeting, said, "I date my first religious impressions from a book handed me by a stranger." It was the means of his and his wife's conversion.

A gentleman meeting a young man, and taking his hand, says, "Christ wants you." He soon after found Christ precious. "The command is, Go speak to that young man." This command is too much neglected. Speak daily to as many as you can. Your power is great as a co-worker with Christ. Take his rule: "Did not our heart burn within us while he talked and opened to us the Scriptures?" Keep the promises constantly before you. This will strengthen your faith and encourage your heart. "But to do good, and to communicate, forget not; for with such sacrifices God is well pleased." Heb. xiii. 16. "Go work in my vineyard." "Every man is rewarded according to what he does." "Never has it entered into the heart of man to conceive the things that are prepared for them that love God." "If the righteous are scarcely saved, where shall the sinner and the ungodly appear?"

---

AFFLICTION. — "Our light affliction, which is but for a moment." Yes, suffering brother or sister, only "for a moment." It may seem long to the weak flesh; but it is only for a little while. Rest will be sweet after the season of toil. Did you never mark the delightful calm that succeeds the violence of the storm? So it will be with the storm of affliction and trial. If faithful, the blessed, eternal calm that shall succeed, will be doubly glorious. We have it as our happy privilege to be made "perfect through suffering." Let us be faithful to the end. "Eye hath not seen, nor ear heard, neither have entered into the heart of man the things which God hath prepared for them that love him."

## NEWSPAPERS AND THEIR INFLUENCE.

At a recent public meeting, held at the American Tract House, the Rev. Mr. Calhoun, from Mt. Lebanon, said that in all Syria, with a population of a million and a half, not a single *newspaper* is published. And in the entire region in which the Arabic language is spoken, comprising Syria, Arabia, Egypt, and the Barbary States, including a population of 40,000,000, there is believed to be only one, if indeed one, newspaper in that language, and only three or four in English or French. There is but one in the Turkish language, in all the Turkish dominions (including a population of 60,000,000), and that conducted by an Englishman. Such facts, he said, afforded an illustration of *Mohammedanism*, — a religion which has no tendency to improvement, either of intellect, morals, or economies.

The first newspaper in the Turkish dominions, as well as in several of the heathen countries, he said, was started by American missionaries. But they are multiplying, and it is an interesting fact that Armenian, Greek, and India journals, as also those of China, Africa, and the Sandwich Islands, are now copying *religious* as well as political intelligence from American daily papers. And it is surely a consummation devoutly to be wished that the impress of pure Christianity be stamped upon all these numberless channels of intelligence, as an example to the nations among whom newspapers are extending.

Who can read the above without offering up the effectual, fervent prayer, that all editors of secular papers and book writers may be brought to a knowledge of Christ; and that the impress of pure Christianity be stamped upon all these numberless channels of intelligence, as an example to all nations. And may the whole church of Christ offer up the effectual, fervent prayer for the outpouring of the Holy Spirit upon this class of our public writers, throughout the whole world; for God is moving among us in a mysterious way. He says, "ask whatsoever you will and it shall be given you." Let us have the faith and zeal of Paul, for the whole world is on the eve of a mighty revolution. Let every Christian see to it that he acts well his part. Some editors of our secular papers devote part of their paper for religious information. They find it costs no more than it does to occupy that space with that which amounts to nothing; they have an increase of business, and we bid them God speed. If all editors would adopt the same rule (with the additional notice of the ·Chapel Prayer Meetings, and their proceedings), then we should reach our business men, who seldom read the Bible, or any religious journal; then we should see a new order of things. Pride, extravagance, and the consumption of time over light reading destroys the influence of the church and the religious press. Our daily papers go to all parts of the world ; and if editors knew the power they have for advancing the cause of Christ, and the happiness that it would give them, and thousands of others, they would devote a part of their paper daily to religious information; there would be no extra expense, for much of the matter in our daily papers is of no account. I say, if they would properly realize this, and exert the influence that the religious press does at the present day, the windows of heaven would open, and God would pour out a blessing upon our churches; and, instead of people resorting to places of amusement, they would crowd our vestries, inquiring the way to eternal life, and this world would become the paradise of God.

The *Messenger and Tract Journal* can be had at No. 28 and 40 Cornhill, for one cent. Let no family, jail, prison, or almshouse be without them; they are worth their weight in gold. There must be a change in our Sabbath school libraries; the story books, which have no Bible foundation, give a tendency to novel reading, that is injurious to the reader and the cause of Christ. There is an abundance of Bible history to furnish a foundation for all the books we require, that can be made interesting to the young, and will lead them on, step by step, towards the pearl of great price. This is the nursery of the church — when this is weakened, the church is. Offer a premium for the best Sabbath school books founded on the Bible. Let the church see to this before it is too late.

---

THE MESSENGER ON THE PRAIRIES. — A cavalry soldier, in Dakotah Territory, found one night, on the Missouri River, some Norwegians, who had a copy of the American Messenger, and lent it to him. He had never before seen the paper, and sat down to read it. " I devoured it," he says, " as a hungry man his dinner. It was food to my weary soul. I was astonished to find it here on this wide prairie, and at so low a price. I have a Christian wife at home and some dear little children. I know they would like to read it, and enclose one dollar, that you may send it to them."

## BLESSED ARE THEY THAT MOURN.

O, DEEM not they are blest alone,
  Whose lives a peaceful tenor keep!
The Power who pities man, has shown
  A blessing for the eyes that weep.

The light of smiles shall fill again
  The lids that overflow with tears,
And weary hours of woe and pain,
  Are promises of happy years.

There is a day of sunny rest
  For every dark and troubled night;
And grief may hide an evening guest,
  But joy shall come with early light.

And thou, who o'er thy friend's low bier
  Sheddest the bitter drops like rain,
Hope that a brighter, happier shore
  Will give him to thy arms again.

Nor let the good man's trust depart,
  Though life its common gift deny;
Though pierced and broken be his heart,
  And spurned of men, he goes to die.

For God has marked each sorrowing day,
  And numbered every secret tear;
And heaven's long age of bliss shall pay
  For all its children suffer here.

## A TRUE GENTLEMAN.

MODERATION, decorum, and neatness distinguish the gentleman. He is at all times affable, diffident, and studious to please; intelligent and polite, his behavior is pleasant and graceful. When he enters the house of an inferior, he endeavors to hide, if possible, the difference between their rank in life. Ever willing to assist those around him, he is neither unkind, haughty, nor overbearing. In the mansions of the great, the correctness of his mind induces him to bend to etiquette, but not to stoop to adulation. Correct principle cautions him to avoid the gaming-table, inebriety, or any other foible that could occasion him self-reproach. Pleased with the pleasures of reflection, he rejoices to see the gayety of society; and is fastidious upon no point of little import. Appear only to be a gentleman, and its shadow will bring upon you contempt; be a gentleman, and its honors will remain after you are dead.

## THE ANGEL OF PATIENCE.

#### A FREE PARAPHRASE OF THE GERMAN.

To weary hearts, to mourning homes,
God's meekest Angel gently comes:
No power has he to banish pain,
Or give us back our lost again;
And yet, in tenderest love, our dear
And heavenly Father sends him here.

There's quiet in that Angel's glance,
There's rest in his still countenance;
He mocks no grief with idle cheer,
Nor wounds with words the mourner's ear.
But ills and woes he may not cure,
He kindly learns us to endure.

Angel of Patience! sent to calm
Our feverish brow with cooling balm;
To lay the storms of hope and fear,
And reconcile life's smile and tear;
The throbs of wounded pride to still,
And make our own our Father's will!

O thou, who mournest on thy way,
With longings for the close of day,
He walks with thee, that Angel kind,
And gently whispers, "Be resigned!
Bear up, bear on; the end shall tell
The dear Lord ordereth all things well!"

## THE LANDING AT CAPE ANN.

The last number of the North American Review thus favorably notices the new contribution to the history of Massachusetts, in a volume lately given to the public by John Wingate Thornton, Esq. Mr. Thornton's book bears the following title: —

"The Landing at Cape Anne: or the Charter of the First Permanent Colony on the Territory of the Massachusetts Company, now discovered and first published from the Original Manuscript. With an Inquiry into its Authority, and a History of the Colony, 1624–1628. Roger Conant, Governor."

This monograph, says the North American, relates to a portion of the history of Massachusetts which has hitherto been somewhat obscure, and especially commemorates the worth, and distinguished services of Roger Conant, whose name ought to lead the list of the Governors of Massachusetts. He came to Plymouth, probably, as early as 1622, and shortly afterward withdrew to Nantasket with a little band of settlers, whose Puritanism was less rigid and exclusive than that of the main body. In 1624 he was invited to serve as governor of a colony established at Cape Ann by the Dorchester Company, who held possession of that tract of territory, as purchasers under a charter granted the previous year to Robert Cushman, Edward Winslow, and their associates at Plymouth. After two years and a half, reverses and discouragements led to the disbanding of the Cape Ann Colony; but Conant, by his prudence and energy, was enabled to retain the best of the planters in the vicinity, removing with them to Naumkeag, now Salem. In 1628 he was superseded by Endicott, under the Massachusetts Bay Charter, and for the remaining half century of his life he no more appears prominently in the affairs of the colony; though his name occurs several times in the records, and in connection with offices and trusts implying the general confidence. He was a man of eminent discretion, gentleness, and probity, though he probably lacked some of the commanding elements of character, as he certainly did the sternness and austerity that marked his successor. He felt, in the latter years of his life, that he was suffering unmerited neglect. In 1630 he had removed to the part of Salem which, in 1668, was incorporated under the name of Beverly

In 1671, with thirty-four others, he petitioned the General Court that this name might be changed for that of his native place, Radleigh; and supported the prayer of said petition by a memorial of his own, commencing as follows: —

"The humble petition of Roger Conant, of Bass River, alias Beverly, who hath bin a planter in New England, fortie yeers and upwards, being one of the first, if not the very first, that resolved and made good any settlement, under God, in matter of plantation, with my family, in this Colony of the Massachusetts Bay, and have bin instrumental both for the founding and carriing on of the same, and when in the infancy thereof it was in great hassard of being deserted. I was a means, through grace assisting me, to stop the flight of those few that were heere with me, and that by my utter deniall to goe away with them, who would have gone either for England, or mostly for Virginia, but thereupon stayed to the hassard of our lives."

We rejoice that justice, though late, has been done to the venerable man, who, as founder and savior of the infant colony, may proffer a double title to a place among the fathers of our Commonwealth. The whole work does credit to Mr. Thornton's zeal as an antiquary, and candor as a historian.

## AN AGED DISCIPLE.

We understand that the last Sabbath completed seventy years since our venerable fellow-citizen, John Punchard, Esq., made a public profession of religion in the Tabernacle Church,[*] of which he has ever since been a most exemplary and respected member. He has been connected with that church during the ministry of six clergyman, viz.: Dr. Whitaker, Mr. Spaulding, Drs. Worcester, senior, Cornelius, Cleveland, and the present pastor, Rev. Dr. S. M. Worcester, who has sustained the pastoral relation for a longer period than either of his predecessors — nearly nineteen years. Mr. Punchard, during his whole life, has been remarkable for constancy and punctuality in his attendance upon public worship, and has undoubtedly listened to more sermons than any person now living among us; and although he has nearly completed his ninetieth year, he still sets an example in this respect

[*] Salem, Mass.

which it would be well for many, who are scores of years his juniors, to imitate. We understand that there are two females living, who have been members of the above church for sixty-five years.

Forty-one years have just elapsed since the first missionaries to the heathen in foreign countries, viz., Samuel Newell, Adoniram Judson, Samuel Nott, Gordon Hall, and Luther Rice were ordained in this country. The ordination took place in the Tabernacle Church, on the 6th of February, 1812. We learn that Dr. Worcester took an appropriate notice of the facts above stated, in his sermon on the last Sabbath, and that his remarks were peculiarly affecting and impressive, — especially those in reference to two youthful disciples, who were then admitted to the church, standing where our venerable friend stood seventy years before, who was now present to rejoice with them in having taken a stand which he took in his youth, and which he had never regretted.

## PREPARATION FOR DEATH.

When you lie down at night, compose your spirits as if you were not to awake till the heavens be no more. And when you awake in the morning, consider that new day as your last, and live accordingly. Surely that night cometh of which you will never see the morning, or that morning of which you will never see the night; but which of your mornings or nights will be such, you know not. Let the mantle of wordly enjoyments hang loose about you, that it may be easily dropped when Death comes to carry you into another world. When the corn is forsaking the ground, it is ready for the sickle; when the fruit is ripe, it falls off the tree easily. So when a Christian's heart is truly weaned from the world, he is prepared for death, and it will be the more easy for him. A heart disengaged from the world is a heavenly one, and then we are ready for heaven when our heart is there before us.

## COUNSEL TO A CLERK.

A young man in New York, who seems to have questioned whether any savings of his would be safe in a Savings Bank, requested the editor of a daily paper to give his judgment whether any pecuniary revulsion, like that of 1837, might be at hand to peril the Savings Banks. The sage editor, having little fear for the Savings Banks, replied, —

"'Merchant's clerk' does well to keep a bright lookout for the future; but if he will eschew stock speculations, fast horses, fast women, costly cigars, mixed drinks, the theatre, and billiard-rooms; will dress economically, spare a portion of his surplus earnings for the gifts of a true charity, and deposit the remainder in a Savings Bank; avoid unprofitable companions, keep the Sabbath, go to bed early, and devote his time, his thoughts, and his energies to the interest of his employers, we will insure him against the effects of the most severe commercial revolution."

## SINGULAR RECOVERY OF A YOUNG LADY GIVEN UP TO DIE.

A MOST singular case of the recovery of a young lady in Fairhaven, Massachusetts, from a long, and apparently fatal illness, is published in the New Bedford Standard, as narrated by the young lady herself. Miss Louisa James, an intelligent and accomplished young lady of twenty-one years, the daughter of widow Mary Mitchell, residing on Rotch Street, Fairhaven, has been ill for the greater part of a year past, and for the last four months she has been confined to her bed. The physicians pronounced her disease one of the heart and lungs, and though the best of medical aid was procured for her, she continued to fail rapidly, and at last it was announced that human skill could do nothing more for her. For the last two months she lost all control of her lower limbs, and it was with the greatest difficulty that she could be moved. She bore her intense sufferings with Christian fortitude. She was reduced so low that her stomach refused the slightest nourishment. On Wednesday, the 8th instant, a female friend visited her, and in the course of a conversation remarked that the Rev. Joseph K. Bellows of New York, of the Second Advent persuasion, to which the invalid belonged, was in town for the purpose of holding a series of meetings. Miss James earnestly desired to see him, and in the evening he called at her residence. She felt that should the reverend gentleman pray for her she should recover, and after a short conversation she made such a request.

The clergyman and the mother of the invalid knelt down, and a fervent and earnest prayer was offered up in her behalf. The mother informs us that before the minister prayed, the body of her daughter was as cold and frigid as marble, and at the close of the exhortation she perspired freely. Miss James describes her sensations during the prayer as similar to those of a person receiving a galvanic shock. That night she passed comfortably, and in the morning she arose and dressed herself without assistance, and on the following Sabbath she attended church. She is now enjoying the best of health, and relishes the heartiest food.

A SMART OLD MAN.— Mr. Nathan Clark, of North Rochester, Massachusetts, aged eighty-eight years and nine months, lately walked from that place to the Head-of-the-River, a distance of eight miles, to visit his friends, without seeming to be much fatigued with his journey. On his eighty-eighth birthday he felled a cord of wood for a present to a needy widow, and in the evening walked three miles to a party given in honor of his pastor, Rev. W. W. Meech. He has never seen a sick day. His food is principally bread, milk, and baked apples; his drink, cold water, which he says "God made, and pronounced good." He is still hale and erect, in the enjoyment of good health, and bids fair to reach over a hundred years. "Go and do likewise."

## A MAN KILLED BY A LION AT ASTLEY'S LONDON AMPHITHEATRE.

At Astley's Amphitheatre, London, on the 7th instant, an undergroom named Smith was literally throttled to death by one of the lions which play so prominent a part in the holiday entertainments at that favorite place of amusement. The lions, three in number, are confined in a cage at the back of the stage. When the night watchman left the theatre in the morning, a few minutes before seven, he reported " all right." Shortly afterwards Smith, the deceased, entered the place and found the lions prowling about. They had torn off a heavy iron bar, which crossed the front of their cage, and then burst open the door. Smith was alone; and not being familiar with the animals, he attempted to escape into an adjoining stable-yard. His situation was a frightful one, and most men would have acted precisely as he did under similar circumstances; but the probability is, that if he had stood his ground boldly, his life would have been saved. Unfortunately, one of the lions — known by the name of Havelock — caught sight of his retreating figure, and instantly sprang upon him. It seized him by the haunches, pulled him to the ground, and then fixed its teeth in his throat. Death must have been almost instantaneous, but as Smith was found a good deal cut up and bruised at the back of the head, it is supposed that the lion, after burying its fangs in his throat, dragged him about, and dashed his head against the ground. There were no cries for help, but a sort of shuffling noise was heard by a man in the stable-yard. He suspected what had occurred, and did not venture to open the door through which Smith had endeavored to escape, but he gave the alarm, and in a few minutes was joined by several grooms and others connected with the theatre. They were all, however, too much afraid to enter the place, and nothing was done to ascertain the fate of Smith until the arrival of Crockett, the Lion Conqueror, to whom the animals belong. As soon as he reached the spot, he passed through the door alone, none of the others daring to follow. The body of Smith was lying face upwards a few feet from the door, and Havelock was crouching over it as a hungry dog crouches over a piece of meat. Crockett immediately threw the animal off, and dragged the body into the yard. It was still warm, but life had been extinct for some time. A surgeon was sent for, but of course he could render no assistance. Crockett lost no time in securing the lions. They allowed him to capture them easily enough. Even Havelock did not offer any resistance, and the other two, which had taken no part in the terrible scene with Smith, seemed rather afraid than otherwise. In a few minutes all three were back in their cage again, and at night they went through their usual performances before a crowded audience.

## COMMERCIAL VALUE OF HONESTY.

An old trader among the Northern Indians, who had some years ago established himself on the Wisseva, tells a good story, with a moral worth recollecting, about his first trials of trading with his red customers. The Indians, who evidently wanted goods, and had both money (which they called *shane ah*) and furs, flooded about his store, and examined his goods, but for some time bought nothing. Finally, their chief, with a large body of his followers, visited him, and accosted him with, "How do, Thomas; show me goods; I take four yard calico, three coon-skins for yard; pay you by'm-by: to-morrow;" received his goods and left. Next day he returned with his whole band, his blanket stuffed with coon-skins. "American man, I pay you now;" with this he began counting him out the skins, until he had handed him over twelve. Then, after a moment's pause, he offered the trader one more, remarking as he did it, "that's it." "I handed it back," said the trader, telling him he owed me but twelve, and I would not cheat him. We continued to pass it back and forth, each one asserting that it belonged to the other. At last he appeared to be satisfied, gave me a scrutinizing look, placed the skins in the fold of his blanket, stepped to the door, gave me a scrutinizing look, and yelled with a loud voice, "Come, come and trade with the pale face; he no cheat Indian; his heart big." He then turned to me and said : "You take that skin; I tell Indian no trade with you — drive you off like dog — but now you Indian friend, and we yours." Before sunrise I was waist deep in furs, and loaded down with cash. So I lost nothing by my honesty.

---

Step in no path, speak no word, commit no act, when conscience appears to whisper "Beware."

## WHAT IS GOD?

What is God? God is a spirit. What is God? God is love. He encampeth about them that love him. He did so in a peculiar manner about George Washington, and used him as an instrument in the salvation of this nation; and now shall we lose it in this present struggle? God forbid! When he informed his pious mother that his nation required his services, her answer was, " Go, George ; " and when she gave him the parting kiss, she goes to her retired room, and prays to God to encamp about him. Her prayer was heard and answered, and our nation was saved.

On his way to receive his commission, who would not like to have looked into that workshop, and see what was going on in that warm heart filled with love for his nation, his fellow-man, and his God? And that deep-rooted principle, that no fiery darts of Satan could remove, and that constant, silent prayer lifting up to God to encamp about him, and for the descent of the Holy Spirit to guide him through all truth, and show him the way. Therefore, what could we expect but God's blessing? And as he goes forward in our nation's struggles, we find him in his winter quarters, needing supplies. After sending to Congress several times, without any definite answer, he supplied his army out of his own money. His soldiers became attached to him, and would not leave him until the close of the war. God encamped about him. One Indian, after firing twenty times with a good rifle, said he was not to be killed with a bullet.

His goodness was not confined to his army. Many a poor family received bread, and did not know the donor. He directed bakers to leave them bread and bring their bill to him. And while at Mount Vernon, God encamped about him there. A gentleman on a visit there noticed that he always left the room at a certain hour. Wishing to know why, he opened the door into the entry, and heard him in another room at prayer. So lived and died this good man. Much more might be said, but enough has been, to show that he was a man after God's own heart.

The Tract Society and the Army. — A donor in Wisconsin writes, "When you see the immense good the American Tract Society has been prepared for and raised up to do in this day of our country's need, I look with veneration on the choice spirits that laid its foundations, and have sustained this great work of Christian benevolence with all its increasing power to do good."

A soldier of the Sixth Pennsylvania cavalry, near Culpepper, Va., referring to an unexpected gift of a messenger while he was wishing for something good to read, says, "My heart leaped for joy. It was to my soul as angels' food to the children of Israel. My soul was greatly blessed while reading it." He sends fifty cents for Messengers for soldiers.

## THE WAR

It is often asked why our present war is not brought to a close. You ask the returned soldier, and he will tell you that if the officers would go forward, the war would soon be brought to a close. They have got to make their pile out of the government; when that is done, they think they will go forward. But it is not so with all. Some are worth their weight in gold, and their names will be handed down through all posterity as an honor to our nation.

The South have been put into the furnace of affliction, and the North have been put in with them for participating with them in their sins. In order to be taken out, we must pay the price. God told the people of Nineveh what the price would be. They paid the price, and were saved. And he has not altered his law. Shall we not do likewise? Jonah delivers his message: " Yet forty days, and you shall

all be destroyed." Hear that heathen monarch to his people: "We will betake ourselves to dust and ashes, and repent of our sins; and who knows but God will forgive us?" "Confess your sins unto God, and he is faithful to forgive." Now, says Jonah, "I shall be mocked." Hear God's answer: "Shall I destroy a people that do not know their right hand from their left, after they have repented in dust and ashes?" They paid the price, and were saved. Shall we be less wise than they, and lose our nation? Reader, you have part of this price to pay yourself: examine the third chapter of Jonah, and see what it is.

---

"PRAY without ceasing." You are a telegraphic spirit. God is at one end of the wire and you at the other. "Whatsoever you ask in faith shall be given you."

## A SEA-CAPTAIN'S OPINION OF NOVELS.

A COLPORTEUR entering the cabin of a large bark, and finding the captain alone, said, "Sir, should you like some religious books for this voyage?"

"Yes, I should; I was formerly a novel-reader, until I found I was becoming crazy. My reading now is religious. I have from time to time read novels all night. Finding I was becoming insane, I gathered up all my novels, opened my cabin window, and gave them a slide into the ocean."

Would not all novel readers do well to gather up all their novels and give them a slide into the fire? Novel-reading betokens a diseased mind, or that of a child. Is it not strange that a person of a well-balanced mind can spend their precious golden moments over light, nonsensical, fictitious reading while in view of the solemn realities of eternity and its unchanging decisions? Is it not because there is no meditation? The Bible command is, "Meditate upon these things." "The ox knows his owner, and the ass his master's crib, but my people do not consider."

You will find on your table a package of letters from your elder brother. "He has gone to prepare a place for you." To enable you to find him, he has directed you to search them daily. It is a revelation from God. The manner in which you receive them will determine your eternal destiny. Have you broke the first seal? When properly studied, it becomes the most interesting of all books. Perhaps you may say you do not understand the doctrine. "He that doeth my will shall know of the doctrine." You know your duty, — do it. You may say that your sins are so numerous they cannot be forgiven. "The blood of Christ cleanseth from all sins." "Confess your sins unto God, and he is faithful to forgive" "Seek and you shall find, knock and it shall be opened unto you." "According to your faith be it done unto you." "Never has it entered into the heart of man to conceive the things that are prepared for them that love God."

Christ has a crown for all that choose to ask. Reader, is it worth asking for? Trusting in the Lord that you have, through his grace, decided to accept of this crown, therefore we would ask a double portion of his divine grace to rest upon you all.

---

A USEFUL HINT TO YOUNG MEN. — For your own comfort, for your friend's solace, for the sake of your eventual prosperity, cultivate a strict and manly habit of economy. It is impossible to raise a good character without it. And this one single article, economy, connected with moderate talent, will recommend you to all from whom you may wish confidence or expect remuneration. Assistance, should you need it, will not be withheld, if it is known that your care of personal expense is correct.

## PRAY FOR EDITORS.

Do ministers and Christians pray as they ought for the editors of the religious and secular press? We fear not. A moment's consideration will show the vast importance of praying for these men.

They exert a mighty influence on society, on churches, on rulers, on governments, and on all the interests of mankind. Their power for good or for evil is incalculable. Pray that this power may always be wisely directed.

To fulfil their high calling faithfully, they need special gifts and qualifications. What wisdom, knowledge, prudence, faith, integrity, courage, firmness, patience, watchfulness, love of truth, God and man, freedom from covetousness, passion, and ambition, they need, that they may sift truth from error, separate the precious from the vile, rebuke the wicked, strengthen the righteous, and never contaminate their columns with any thing that is impure or pernicious! Pray for them, that they may be endowed with every requisite gift.

## BE IN EARNEST.

WHERE there is deadness in a man's own soul, there is not likely to be much vitality in his work; and where there is little vitality, there will also, in all human probability, be but little success. When a man is not *in earnest* about a thing, he is easily discouraged; he will not try again and again; he will not *determine* (God willing) that it *shall* be done. When a man is in earnest about a thing, he brings every resource at his command to bear upon it; he tries one way, and if that do not succeed, he tries another; let that fail, he tries something else, and very seldom indeed does the earnest man finally miss success. When a man is not earnest, every little impediment forms an insuperable obstacle; this thing and that thing, which others make scarcely any account of, he cannot get over at all; and this is the reason why so many Sunday school teachers drop off when they have tried the work for a little while.

## THE COLPORTEUR'S TREAT.

A COLPORTEUR in Southern New York says, "One stormy day I drove my horse into a wagon-house attached to a back country tavern, and taking my carpet-bag, passed into the bar-room, which was full. I sat by the fire to warm and dry my clothes, when I was slapped very familiarly on the shoulder, the friendly salute being followed by the intimation that I should 'treat,' as it was the rule of that house that every new-comer should treat the company. I replied that I would, when they all with one accord rushed to the bar. I hurriedly requested them to wait a little for me. I then drew out a handful of tracts, and supplied each of them with one, accompanying it with such counsel as I thought the recipient needed. The result was, the liquor was untasted, and I was troubled with no further requests to 'treat.'"

## INFLUENCE OF THE MESSENGER.

The pastor of a feeble church in Western New York, says that, chiefly by the efforts of a benevolent lady, they have been encouraged to form a library for the use of the people, and adds, " You are aware that this church has for two years past paid seventy-five dollars, annually, into your treasury. Such a thing was never before done here, and it is the result of the circulation of the Messenger, and of encouraging the people to little exertions, one after another, until at length, after four years, instead of receiving aid from the Board of Domestic Missions to sustain the institutions of the gospel among themselves, they are this year building a fine new church, and giving about two hundred dollars to benevolent purposes. We regard the establishment of this library as another lever applied to the right spot to raise the people to more enlarged views, and more efficient coöperation in every good work. God's Spirit is awakening them to take their part in the evangelization of the world."

## ONE VOYAGE MORE.

"I WILL make but one voyage more," said Captain Seymour to his wife, who was urging him to abandon the perils of the sea, and to give that attention to the education of his children, which their age and circumstances required.

"You have made too many already," replied Mrs. S. "Your life is of too much consequence to your family to be needlessly put in peril."

"I am sorry to leave you and the children; but as to peril, we are just as safe at sea as on land."

"A great many are lost at sea."

"And a great many die on land."

"But they do not die violent deaths."

"Well, I promise you this shall be my last voyage. I will settle down, and devote myself to my family."

Why did he not do so at once? His children needed a father's care. He had sufficient property to meet his reasonable wants. He loved his wife and children with an ardent love; why did he not remain with them?

He wished to add a little more to his property, as does almost every one who has made any. Besides, he loved the excitement of the sea; loved to tread the quarter-deck as master.

He set out on a voyage, and was never heard of more. Never, till the sea gives up her dead, will the fate of the good ship Medusa be known.

This family were not without the means of support, but they were without a head and director. The boys soon passed beyond the control of their gentle mother, and became wild, wicked, reckless.

Had their father relinquished the sea when urged to do so by his wife, his boys might have been trained aright; for he was a man of rare energy, and knew how to govern and to influence.

How many lose their souls by resolving to make one sinful adventure more! They will once more indulge in forbidden pleasure! They will once more yield to temptation, and then they will devote themselves to the service of God!

How many who do not go down to the sea in ships suffer their families to go to ruin, in their efforts to make one successful speculation more!

The temporal and eternal happiness of one's family is more important than a commercial adventure. To train one's children aright, is far more important than to accumulate a fortune for them.

---

A COLPORTEUR in Michigan recently received a donation of fifty dollars, to be divided between the Home and Foreign Missionary and the Tract Societies. It was the balance of one thousand dollars, which had been consecrated to the Lord by a gentleman from California, being one third of his gains.

## THE FAMILY RODS.

BEREAVEMENT — this is the bitterest of all earthly sorrows. It is the sharpest arrow in the quiver of God. To love tenderly and deeply, and then to part; to meet together for the last time on earth; to bid farewell for time; to have all past remembrances of home and kindred broken up; this is the reality of sorrow. To look upon that face that shall smile upon us no more; to close those eyes that shall see us no more; to press those lips that shall speak to us no more; to stand by the cold side of father, mother, brother, sister, friend, yet hear no sound and receive no greeting; to carry to the tomb the beloved of our hearts, and then to return to a desolate home with a blank in one region of our souls, which shall never again be filled till Jesus come with all his saints; — this is the bitterness of grief; this is the wormwood and the gall!

It is the rod which ever and anon God is laying upon us. Nor is there any that we need more than this. By it, he is making room for himself in hearts that had been filled with other objects and engrossed with other loves. He is jealous of our affection, for he claims it all as his own; and every idol he will utterly abolish. For our sakes as well as for his own he can suffer no rival in the heart. Perhaps the joys of an earthly home are stealing away our hearts from the many mansions above. God breaks. in upon us in mercy,-and turns that home into a wilderness. Our sin finds us out; we mourn over it and seek anew to realize our heavenly citizenship, and set out anew upon our pilgrim way; alone, and yet not alone, for the Father is with us. Perhaps we are sitting " at ease in Zion," comfortable and contented, amid the afflictions of a suffering church and the miseries of ·a world that owns no Saviour and fears no God. Jehovah speaks and we awake. He takes to himself some happy saint, or smites to the dust some wretched sinner. We are troubled at the stroke. We mourn our lethargy.

While we slept a fellow-saint has gone up to be with Christ, and a fellow-sinner has gone down to be with the devil and his angels. The death of the one stirs us up, the death of the other solemnizes and overawes us.

Thus as saint after saint ascends to God, we begin to feel that heaven is far more truly the family home than earth. We have far more brethren above than we have below. And each bereavement reminds us of this. It reminds us, too, that the coming of the Lord draweth nigh, and makes us look out more wistfully from our eastern casement for the first streaks of the rising dawn. It kindles in us strong desires for the day of happy meeting in our Father's house, when we shall clasp inseparable hands, and climb in company the everlasting hills. Meanwhile it bids us give our hearts to Jesus only. It does for us what the departure of the two strangers from heaven did to the disciples on the mount of transfiguration; — it leaves us alone with Jesus. It turns into deep experience that longing for home contained in the apostle's words, " having a desire to depart and to be with Christ, which is far better."

The more that bereavement transforms earth into a desert, the more are our desires drawn up to heaven. Our treasures having been transferred to heaven, our hearts must follow them. Earth's hopes are smitten, and we are taught to look for " that blessed hope, the glorious appearing of the great God and Saviour Jesus Christ." The night is falling and the flowers are folding up; but as they do so they bid us look upward and see star after star coming out upon the darkening sky.

---

A NEW sect has been formed in Wurtemburg under the name of " Friends of Jerusalem," and with the object of reconstructing the Temple of Jerusalem, so as to fulfil the prophecies. It has already sent out a commission to undertake the rebuilding of the Temple of Solomon, but it has only been able to raise five thousand four hundred and twenty florins for the purpose.

## THE MOTHER'S LAST LESSON.

" Will you please teach me my verse, mamma, and then kiss me, and bid me good night?" said little Roger L., as he opened the door and peeped cautiously into the chamber of his sick mother. "I am very sleepy, but no one has heard me say my prayers."

Mrs. L. was very ill; indeed, her attendants believed her to be dying. She sat propped up with pillows, and struggling for breath; her lips were white; her eyes were growing dull and glazed, and the purple blood was settling at the ends of her cold, attenuated fingers. She was a widow, and little Roger was her only, her darling child. Every night he had been in the habit of coming into her room and sitting upon her lap, or kneeling by her side, while she repeated to him passages from God's Holy Word, or related to him stories of the wise and good men spoken of in its pages. She had been in delicate health for many years, but never too ill to learn little Roger his verse and hear his prayers.

"Hush! hush!" said a lady, who was watching beside her couch, "your dear mamma is too ill to hear you say your prayers to-night. I will put you in bed;" and as she said this, she came forward and laid her hand gently upon his arm, as though she would have led him from the room. Roger began to sob as if his little heart would break.

"I cannot go to bed without saying my prayers — indeed, I cannot!"

The ear of the dying mother caught the sound. Although she had been nearly insensible to every thing transpiring around her, the sound of her darling's sobs aroused her from her stupor, and turning to a friend, she desired her to bring him to her couch and lay him on her bosom. Her request was granted, and the child's rosy cheek and golden head nestled beside the pale cold face of his dying mother. Alas, poor fellow! how little did he realize then the irreparable loss which he was soon to sustain!

"Roger, my son, my darling child," said the dying mother, " repeat this verse after me, and never, *never* forget it : ' *When my father and my mother forsake me, then the Lord will take me up.*' " The child repeated it distinctly, and said his little prayer. He then kissed the cold, almost rigid lips before him, and went quietly to his little couch.

When he arose in the morning, he sought, as usual, his mother's room, but he found her cold and still! — wrapped in her winding sheet! That was her last lesson! He has never forgotten it! — he probably never will! He has grown to be a man, — a *good* man, — and now occupies a post of much honor and distinction in Massachusetts. I never could look upon him without thinking about the faith so beautifully exhibited by his dying mother. It was not misplaced. The Lord has taken her darling up.

If you have *God* for your friend, you need *never fear ;* father and mother may forsake you — the world may seem to you like a dreary waste, full of pit-falls and thorns — but he can bring you safely through trials, and give you at last a golden harp and snowy robe, like those the purified wear in heaven. He can even surround your death-bed by angel visitants. He is all-powerful — an ever-present help in time of trouble. Will you not, then, seek his friendship and keep his commandments?

DESTITUTION IN NEW YORK. — A colporteur in Northern New York writes, "I visited a family in a log hut that had no Bible, or any religious books or tracts, until I supplied them. The woman said that her husband had been to meeting twice in three years. She had kept house nine years. Another told me she had not been to a meeting in three years; and another, that she had only been to meeting twice in four years, and that she had no Bible or religious books. Many similar facts I might mention."

## POWER OF RELIGION.

The following anecdote, selected from an English paper, is said to have been related by a clergyman who was acquainted with the facts:—

Lord —— was a man of the world. His pleasures were drawn from his riches, his honors, and his friends. His daughter was the idol of his heart. Much had been expended for her education; and well did she repay, in her intellectual endowments, the solicitude of her parents. She was highly accomplished, amiable in her disposition, and winning in her manners. They were both strangers to God.

At length Miss —— attended a Dissenter's meeting in London; was deeply awakened, and soon happily converted. Now she was delighted in the service of the sanctuary and social meetings. To her the charms of Christianity were overflowing. She frequented those places where she met with congenial minds, animated with similar hopes.

The change was marked by her fond father with painful solicitude. To see his lovely daughter thus infatuated, was to him an occasion of deep grief; and he resolved to correct her erroneous notions on the subject of the real pleasure and business of life. He placed at her disposal large sums of money, hoping she would be induced to go into the fashions and extravagances of others of her birth, and leave the meetings. But she maintained her integrity. He took her long journeys, and conducted in the most engaging manner, in order to divert her mind from religion; but she still delighted in the Saviour.

After failing in many projects, which he fondly anticipated would be effectual, he introduced her into company under circumstances that she must either join in the recreation of the party or give offence. Hope lighted up in the countenance of this affectionate but misguided father, as he saw his snare about to entangle the object of his solicitude. It had been arranged among his friends that several young ladies, on the approaching festive occasion, should give a song, accompanied by the pianoforte.

The hour arrived; the party assembled. Several had performed their parts to the great delight of the party, which was in high spirits. Miss —— was now called on for a song, and many hearts now beat high in hopes of victory. Should she decline, she was disgraced; should she comply, their triumph was complete. This was the moment to seal her fate! With perfect self-possession, she took her seat at the pianoforte, and run her fingers over its keys, and commenced playing and singing, in a sweet air, the following words: —

> "No room for mirth or trifling here,
> For worldly hope or worldly fear,
>   If life so soon is gone;
> If now the Judge is at the door,
> And all mankind must stand before
>   Th' inexorable throne!

> "No matter which my thoughts employ,
>   A moment's misery or joy;

> But O! when both shall end,
> Where shall I find my destined place?
> Shall I my everlasting days,
> With fiends or angels spend?"

She arose from her seat. The whole party was subdued. Not a word was spoken. One by one left the house. Her father wept aloud. Lord —— never rested until he became a Christian. He lived an example of Christian benevolence, having given to benevolent Christian enterprises, before his death, nearly half a million of dollars.

---

PROCRASTINATION. — Near the close of his life, Patrick Henry laid his hand on the Bible, and said to a friend, "Here is a book worth more than all others; yet it is my misfortune never to have read it with proper attention until lately." William Pitt, when he came to die, said, "I fear that I have, like many others, neglected my religious duties too much to have any ground to hope that they can be efficacious on my death-bed."

## WORDS FITLY SPOKEN.

During a revival in a New England female seminary some years ago, one pupil was singled out as an especial subject of prayer. She was not only indifferent, but an open scoffer. No appeals moved her, no entreaties softened her. The faith of some praying hearts wavered; not that of the godly principal of the school.

God's ways are not our ways, thought she, and went on striving and praying. One morning, during the precious season, she chose for her devotional exercises the fifth chapter of first Peter. "The devil, as a roaring lion, walketh about seeking whom he may devour," fell from her lips with solemn emphasis. God sped the arrow. The words smote that sinful girl's heart, and she was brought to the feet of Jesus.

---

Family expenses and annual subscriptions are like revolutions. They never go backwards.

## PRIDE.

"THE pride of life is not of the Father, but is of the world." — 1 *John* ii. 16.

"Pride is a double traitor, and betrayeth itself to entrap thee, making thee vain of thy self-knowledge, and proud of thy discoveries of pride." — *Tupper.*

"As cankers breed in the sweetest roses, so pride may arise out of the sweetest duties." — *Mason.*

"If at any time you have enlargement in prayer, and are favored with access to the throne of grace, do not go away satisfied and self-complacent. Pride says, 'I have done very well now; God will accept this.' You, perhaps, discover that this is the suggestion of pride; it then takes a new turn. Another would not have discovered it to be pride; I must be very humble to see it thus. Thus, if you continue the search, you will find pride like the different coats of an onion, lurking one beneath another to the very centre." — *Payson.*

" A man's lawful pride includes humility."— *Young.*

> " Though various foes against the truth combine,
> Pride, above all, opposes her design;
> Pride of a growth superior to the rest,
> The subtlest serpent, with the loftiest crest,
> Swells at the thought, and, kindling into rage,
> Would hiss the cherub Mercy from the stage." — *Cowper.*

" Blessed is the man that respecteth not the proud." — *Psalms* xl. 4.

> "How poor a thing is Pride! when all, as slaves
> Differ but in their fetters, not their graves." —*Daniel.*

" Jesus was humble, and angels are humble; only devils and fallen men are proud." — *Pike.*

"Pride is the worst viper that is in the human heart, the greatest disturber of the soul's peace and of sweet communion with Christ. It was the first sin committed, and lies lowest in the foundation of Satan's whole building, and is with greatest difficulty rooted out; and is the most hidden, secret, and deceitful of all lusts, and often creeps insensibly into the midst of religion, even, sometimes, under the disguise of humility itself." — *Jonathan Edwards.*

> "Pride, self-adoring pride, was primal cause
> Of all sin past, all pain, all woe to come." — *Pollok.*

"A high look and a proud heart is sin." — *Proverbs* xxi. 4.

---

NEVER stay away from meeting without an excuse that will stand the test at the judgment-day.

## THE NOVEL READER.

All day long Marcia sat in the corner of the family-room reading a novel. So absorbed was she, it was hard to lay it down to take her meals even. Her mother was obliged to speak more than once if she wished her assistance in any thing, and if at last she succeeded by an exercise of authority in making her do what she was at first requested to, she went to the work with a sullen tragic air, as if she was the fancied heroine of her story, enduring all manner of persecutions and fanciful distresses.

Aunt Anne, who was but a visitor in the house, took note of all this, but wisely said that it was useless to comment, until the heroine was fairly brought out of all her tribulations and desirably settled in life; then Marcia might be willing to hear something besides her story. It was ended, at last, and with a dissatisfied air the young lady put it aside and came down to every-day life again. Never did the stocking-basket, with its overflowing contents, look so distasteful to her as after her just taking her departure from such enchanting scenes, fragrant with orange buds, and fluttering with gossamer robes and bridal veils.

"Do you feel that your time has been profitably spent to-day?" asked practical aunt Annie, "and does novel reading make you any happier, Marcia?"

"I'm sure it makes me a great deal happier while I am reading it, Aunt Annie, and there are a great many lovely sentiments in this book, and real religious truth is inculcated at times. I think it is a real good book, and you would think so too, if you would read it, I feel sure."

"What would you think of a miller, Marcia, who would look over handful by handful a bushel of chaff for a few grains of wheat which might possibly be scattered among it, when there were great golden granaries at his hand which were quite free to him. Where there is such a world of real, elevating, excellent literature, which will help to refine you, to fit you for a high intellectual position, and fit your soul for eternity, what a waste it seems to spend your hours over what unfits you for all this — over reading which weakens your mind, which, if long continued, will make you a silly sentimentalist, instead of a woman of culture and sound judgment, whose opinions are received with respect and confidence.

"Above all, my dear girl, such reading hardens the heart. The more we weep over imaginary sorrows, the less we shall sympathize with real ones. It deadens the soul, too. The habitual novel reader cannot be also a Bible reader — cannot be a prayerful Christian. Is this enjoyment worth the loss of the soul, Marcia?"

---

NEVER be proud. "God gives grace to the humble, but knows the proud afar off."

## FASHIONABLE CALL.

Enter Miss Lucy, nearly out of breath with the exertion of walking from her papa's carriage in the street to the door of her friend.

*Lucy.* — "O Marie! how do you do? How delighted I am to see you! How have you been since you were at the ball last Thursday evening? O, wasn't the appearance of that tall girl in pink perfectly frightful? Is this your shawl on the piano? Beautiful shawl! Father says he is going to send to Paris to get me a shawl in the spring. I can't bear homemade shawls! How do you like Monsieur Esprey? Beautiful man, ain't he? Now, don't laugh, Marie, for I am sure I don't care any thing about him! O, my! I must be going! It's a beautiful day, isn't it? Marie, when are you coming up to see me? O, dear! what a beautiful pin! That pin was given to you; now I know it was, Marie; don't deny it. Harry is coming up to see me this evening, but I hate him — I do really; but he has a beautiful mustache, hasn't he, Marie? O, dear, it's very warm. Good morning, Marie! Don't speak of Harry in connection with my name to any one; for I am sure it will never amount to any thing, but I hate him awfully — I'm sure I do. Adieu."

How to ascertain the Health of the Lungs. — Draw in as much breath as possible; then count without drawing in more, till the lungs are exhausted. In consumption, the time does not exceed ten, and is frequently less than six seconds. In pleurisy and pneumonia it ranges from nine to four seconds. When the lungs are in a sound condition, the time will range as high as from twenty to thirty-five seconds.

Truth is like steam; the more it is compressed the greater is its force of expansion.

## THE BEST SERMON.

We are too often ready to judge that to be the best sermon which has many strange thoughts in it, many fine hints, and some grand and polite sentiments. But a Christian, in his best temper of mind, will say, "That is a good sermon which brings my heart nearer to God, which makes the grace of Christ sweet to my soul, and the commands of Christ easy and delightful. That is an excellent discourse, indeed, which enables me to mortify some unruly sin, to vanquish a strong temptation, and weans me from all the enticements of this lower world; that which bears me up above all the disquietudes of life, which fits me for the hour of death, and makes me ready and desirous to appear before Christ Jesus my Lord." — *Preface to Dr. Watts's Sermons.*

Who can read the above and desire a better model for a sermon. It reminds us of Dr.

Griffin's manner of preaching, which was to preach to the heart and conscience of his hearers. He preached as a dying man to dying men; and it came from the heart and it reached the hearts of his hearers, and no other sermon will. If a sermon does not come from the heart of the speaker, it is of but little account. Dr. Griffin encouraged more individual effort for the cause of Christ, and kept constantly before him the manner of Christ's preaching on the Mount. This was the means of his success. If all our clergy should adopt this rule, we should soon see a new order of things. Let the whole church of Christ offer up the effectual, fervent prayer that the entire clergy may have a fresh baptism of the Holy Spirit, and put off cold formality and put on Christ and him crucified. Our nation is in mourning. One calamity follows another. Where is there a family that there is not one dead? "God is doing a quick work on the earth." "The ox knows his owner, and the ass his master's crib, but my people doth not consider."

## DANIEL WEBSTER ON PREACHING.

JOHN ANGELL JAMES has a letter in The British Banner, consisting of comments on the remarks of Daniel Webster, which have gone the rounds, touching the kind of preaching which he professed. The paragraph of Webster which Mr. James especially commends is this: —

"If clergymen in our day would return to the simplicity of the gospel, and preach more to individuals and less to the crowd, there would not be so much complaint of the decline of true religion. Many of the ministers of the present day take their texts from St. Paul and preach from the newspapers. When they do so, I prefer to enjoy my own thoughts rather than to listen. I want my pastor to come to me in the spirit of the gospel, saying, 'You are mortal; your probation is brief; your work must be done speedily. You are immortal, too. You are hastening to the bar of God!

the Judge standeth before the door.' When I am thus admonished, I have no disposition to muse or to sleep. These topics, said Mr. Webster, have often occupied my thought; and if I had time, I would write upon them myself."

He says that when such a man delivers his views of the pulpit, it becomes those who occupy it to listen with deference; and he says that his judgment is sound, rational, and Scriptural, and in harmony with the same order of minds in general; that it is a mistake to suppose that great men go to hear sermons, wishing to hear something profound or eloquent, or matter to engage, at the full stretch, their own imperial understandings. But sometimes ministers overlook the wants of the great body of their people to get something lofty for these individuals of loftier mould, and then produce just what these individuals do not want. And generally, he thinks, the more intelligent part of the congregation, after a week's labor, amid the cares and perplexities of business, come to the sanctuary for something better than the dry crust of philosophical research or profound intellectuality. They want to be made *to feel*, as well as think; they want something for the heart, as well as for the understanding; to have their connection with eternity kept before their minds, and their whole souls stirred up to prepare for it. They feel as if they had been losing their souls amid the anxieties of the world, and they wish to be brought in view of things unseen and eternal. Of course we want less of elaboration and straining after greatness and novelty in our preaching, and more of simplicity, spirituality, and unction; less of the wisdom of words, and more of the doctrines of the Cross, in its Scriptural clearness and unadorned glory.

Another important quality of preaching is commended in these remarks: that is, individuality in the aims of the preacher. Christ did not address congregations as such, but made the individual feel that he was speaking to him, and that he must stand or fall alone —

must live, and die, and give account for himself. Though a preacher must deal in discussions and in general instruction, and though he cannot always be hortatory, he should preach, not only before his hearers, but to them. He ought not to be personal, but he should be so characteristic, as that every conscience should feel that he is searching it. He should place his hearers apart, and prevent their losing themselves in the crowd. He must make them think of *themselves* while in the crowd, as they will do in the day of judgment.

We want power to awaken the conscience from its deep slumber. Never was this power more wanted than now, to bear down the overwhelming influence of trade, pleasure, and knowledge, the prevailing taste for which, is swallowing up the hearts of the people, and rendering our preaching abortive. We must arise and bestir ourselves, for we have too much cause to utter the complaint of the prophet: "There is none that calleth upon Thy name, that stirreth up himself to take hold of thee."

## THE MINISTRY WE NEED.

A PROFESSOR in one of our theological seminaries writes as follows: " The greatest wants in our ministry are zeal and skill in preaching. We want powerful, popular *preachers*. Mere learning, however sound, and piety, however ardent, will avail but little without zeal and tact in preaching." This just and important sentiment we commend to the attention of our candidates for the gospel ministry. " God has ordained, by the foolishness of *preaching*, to save them that believe." Though the *matter* of our preaching stands first in importance, very much depends on the *manner;* by which we mean now, not rhetorical style of composition, or eloquent delivery, but *zeal* and *tact;* that zeal which is the fruit of *ardent love for souls;* and that tact (not artifice) which is implied in the phrase "*wise to win souls.*" These qualities, as distinguished from " mere learning, however sound, and piety, however ardent," we would characterize as consisting in the *union* of solid learning and ardent piety, and in their being employed *zealously and skilfully* in the work of *preaching*. The pulpit is not the place to *display* learning, yet learning may be used there with great effect, if controlled and sanctified by ardent piety. But again, ardent piety connected with learning may be so deficient in the requisite *energy and tact* as to fail in making " powerful and popular *preachers*."

To be " *powerful and popular*," in the sense of the correspondent (we speak from our knowledge of the man whose preaching possesses both of these characteristics), there must be strong good sense, evangelical theology, sound argument, apposite Scripture quotations and illustrations ; and our sermons must be delivered with hearts glowing with earnest emotion, with lips touched, like Isaiah's, with a live coal from the altar, and with tongues as " the pen of a ready writer." We do not assert that these qualities can be attained in an equal degree by all. But if our candidates for the ministry will keep them constantly in view, and diligently apply themselves to their attainment, they will at least attain them so far as to add greatly to the power and effectiveness of their pulpit ministrations. To *preach* is to make *proclamation*, like a public crier; and we have in the ministry of John the Baptist, to whom this term is applied, a forcible illustration of its import when used to describe a preacher of the gospel. We hope that all who are looking to the sacred office will become, in power and spirit, *John Baptists — faithful harbingers* of Christ; proclaiming boldly, earnestly, and effectively, "*Prepare ye the way of the Lord.*"

---

THE first great thing in religion is, to receive Christ; the second is, to live upon him; the third is, to walk in him; the last, to be forever with him.

## ENCOURAGEMENT TO THE AFFLICTED.

Be always ready to give an encouraging word to the afflicted. Who has not been comforted by some good Samaritan while passing through deep waters? Christ has given an example: "Blessed are the poor in spirit, for theirs is the kingdom of heaven." "Blessed are they that mourn, for they shall be comforted." "Blessed are the meek, for they shall inherit the earth." "Blessed are they which do hunger and thirst after righteousness, for they shall be filled." "Blessed are the merciful, for they shall obtain mercy." "Blessed are the pure in heart, for they shall see God." "Blessed are the peacemakers, for they shall be called the children of God." "Blessed are they which are persecuted for righteousness' sake, for theirs is the kingdom of heaven." "Ye are the salt of the earth." "Ye are the light of the world." "Let your light so shine before men, that they may see your good works, and glorify your Father which is in heaven." "If you love me, you will keep my commandments." "All things work together for good to them that love God." "He that loveth not, knoweth not God, for God is love." "Beloved, if God so loved us, we ought also to love one another." "We love him, because he first loved us." "By this we know that we love the children of God, when we love God, and keep his commandments." "God is love, and he that dwelleth in love dwelleth in God, and God in him." "There is no fear in love, but perfect love casteth out fear." Read the first Epistle of John.

A THANK-OFFERING. — A German colporteur in Missouri, sending ten dollars, says, "The enclosed amount would have been expended for the funeral of our child had it died, but God has restored it to us from the grave."

A QUERY.— Was any soul ever converted by looking at *another's* sins?

## OLD SOUTH CHAPEL PRAYER-MEETING, AND ITS INFLUENCE,

Now held in Tremont Temple. The hour in the winter from half past eight to half past nine, in the summer from eight to nine. Some bring in others with them; would not all do well to adopt the same rule? Any one having ten minutes to spare would do well to attend. As Dr. Jenks and another gentleman were going up the steps, with their hearing trumpets, two clerks opposite remarked, "What is there in the chapel so attractive? they must be nearly eighty years old; would they not do well to go and see?"

They are going up to take another draught at the same fountain where they have so often been refreshed. From a gentleman that attends those meetings, we gather the following:—

In the first place, they have adopted the three-minute rule. The hymn-book is seldom used. In a few minutes you hear from all parts of the chapel. If you have one spark of grace in your heart, it will soon be kindled to a lively flame. From one you hear, 'The hour I spent here is the happiest hour of my life;' from another, 'They have got something here I have not got; I wish I could get it.' Would it not be well for us all to go there, and find out what they have got. Take a village prayer-meeting: A brother is called upon to lead in prayer; he prays nearly fifteen minutes; he prays you into a good spirit, and prays you out of it. One rises to encourage more individual effort; his remarks are good. A hymn is read and sung. One more long prayer, then comes the doxology, and the meeting is closed.

If they should adopt this rule at the Chapel, how many would there be besides the sexton? I leave that for others to answer. My object has been to encourage a better attendance at our village prayer-meetings. This stereotype form must be done away with. Our Methodist brethren have, and a blessing has followed; we bid them God speed. In order to have

God's blessing on our churches, there must be a short, effectual, fervent prayer, coming from the heart. Then it will reach the heart of others (having singing and exhortation to correspond). We shall then hear from all parts of the vestry a rapid exchange of thought, from many that we never heard before, and partake of that spirit we so much admire at the Chapel.

O, may the day be not far distant when all our prayer meetings will be filled with anxious inquirers for the way of eternal life. Then they will bear some resemblance to that upper room, where they were all of one heart and mind. And may God, in his tender mercy, give all our churches a double portion of his divine grace, and this world become the paradise of God.

Read the following : —

"A LETTER FROM SOUTH AUSTRALIA.

"The following letter was received at our office during the past week. The writer seems, from one expression, to be a clergyman. He, through our journal, has heard of the answers that God has given to the petitions of his people who have assembled at the Old South Chapel. He has such confidence in the prayers here uttered, that he has sent half round the globe to enlist their petitions in behalf of a prodigal son. This letter will speak to the heart of every parent who has impenitent children.

" The writer evidently mistakes the person to whom the letter is addressed for the pastor of the Old South Chapel."

MITCHEN, NEAR ADELAIDE, SO. AUSTRALIA,
August 31, 1858.

REV. MARTIN MOORE, Old South Chapel, Boston.

DEAR CHRISTIAN BROTHER: Although I have never seen you in the flesh, or your country, or the good people among whom God has so very frequently poured such fulness of blessing and spread such a table, yet permit me, though a stranger, while God is so blessing the provision of his house, and satisfying you all with bread, to crave, as a poor Gentile dog, a crumb of mercy for my poor lost and far off son, given up to drunken habits, thus losing his precious time and precious ability, which is his by natural advantages, by the opening of a kind providence, and by education,— all now lost by the power of his besetting sin. O sirs and brothers! if you can, by your united petitions at the throne of Jesus, do any thing for us, have compassion and help us.

I have been led to take this extraordinary step, from the conduct of the saints of old. They are said to look on the right hand where he doth work. Again, those who come to Jesus did not meet with any rebuff, when they cried, They are worthy for whom he should do this. Also the success many among you have had lately,— I refer to what you relate respecting the mother's advice to her son, to be at the prayer-meeting at twelve o'clock,* &c. Blessed

---

* This, we suppose, has reference to a fact published in the Recorder last spring. A pious mother in the country had a son who was going to New York to seek business. She extorted a promise from him that he would attend the

be the Lord for such tokens! O Lord, hear our prayer, and let our cry come unto him in an acceptable time, when thou mayst be found; and likewise, I may add, the challenge of God, — "Prove me now herewith; the declaration and council for all these things will I be inquired of," &c. And "ask and ye shall receive, that your joy may be full." And "if two or three of you agree to ask any thing in my name, it shall be done."

Now, my dear sir, I feel as weak as water; I do deserve reproof in the matter, and feel also, and cry, "Lord, I believe, help thou my unbe-

---

Fulton Street prayer-meeting at twelve o'clock every day. He went to the city, did not find any lawful business, but found the card table. In the midst of a game the clock struck twelve, and he flung down his cards, and said that he had an engagement of honor that he must fulfil. His companions said, "Play out the game." He replied, "No. I promised my mother that I would attend the business men's prayer-meeting at Fulton Street every day, and I shall go." "You go to a prayer-meeting." "Yes, I shall go to a prayer-meeting." All his companions accompanied him, and within one week he and they were converted.

lief." Yea, I am unworthy that Jesus, or the Spirit, should come under my roof. I know that other children's souls are as dear to God as my child's, but, O, sir, may the utterance be allowed, "*My son! My son!*" "Sir, come down ere my son, my child, die."

> " 'Tis his the lost sinner to save and renew.
> Faith, mighty, beginner and finisher too."

O, my dear sir, and O, you highly favored, grant me this request, my earnest desire, and entreat the Lord for me, and may he say, in answer to your prayer, Bring thy son hither *to me*. O, what a morn! O, what music in heaven! O, what joy in my soul, in my family, in and among the people with whom I labor! O, what a new world he will be ushered into! God, for Christ's sake, grant it, and return you unspeakable blessings for this your kindness, and still keep you all near the throne of grace, and bring you faultless before the throne of glory. Amen.        Yours, &c.,

G. P.

## SPECIFIC PRAYER.

MANY prayers are offered by Christians, to which they apparently never realize an answer, for the reason, doubtless, that they are too general in their character. It is the "effectual, fervent prayer of the righteous man" which "availeth much." But from the very nature of the human mind it is impossible that such a prayer can be offered up for *things in general*. It is only for special favors — definite objects — that the mind can be intensely interested. That object, it is true, may be of very general interest, and an answer to the petition may be a very general blessing, and yet be none the less definite; as, for instance, the outpouring of God's Spirit upon a church or community, resulting in a great and general revival of religion. In that case, the petition may take the form, "O Lord, revive thy work," and may come from a heart intensely desiring the blessing. But for a blessing in general, without any definite object as to the location or character of it, it is simply impossible for any human mind to pray fervently or importunately — two essential elements in prevailing prayer.

It is a fact, which cannot have escaped the notice of the attentive reader of the New Testament, that all the petitions which were presented to the Saviour in the days of his flesh, or which were commended by him, were very specific. Bartimeus cries, " Jesus, thou Son of David, have mercy on me." The special blessing which he wanted was, " that I may receive my sight." The centurion desired the healing of his servant. The Syro-Phœnician woman's errand to the Saviour was the healing of her daughter. The publican's prayer, which the Saviour commended as a model, was, " God be merciful to me a sinner." They were definite objects which these persons brought to a throne of grace, and they brought them because they felt an intense interest in them, and ardently desired the blessings which they sought, and therefore prayed for them with an earnestness and importunity which would take no denial. All the petitions thus presented to the Son of God were heard and graciously answered.

The same fact is seen in the answers to prayer, of which we hear almost daily, in connection with the union prayer-meetings in this city, in New York, and other places. A parent presents the case of an impenitent son, perhaps at a distance from home; a wife asks prayer for the conversion of an ungodly husband; another for a friend upon a bed of death, etc. And often, very often, are we cheered with the information that those who have been made the objects of these special petitions are either under conviction or rejoicing in hope. Why is it that these prayer-meetings differ so much in their visible results from ordinary prayer-meetings? Not, certainly, because of any "variableness" in the Hearer and Answerer of prayer. He is "the same yesterday, to-day, and forever." The same to one petitioner as to another, under the same circumstances. No " praying breath " for things agreeable to his will is ever " spent in vain." But it is because where there is a definite object presented there is concert of desire as well as prayer. " If two of you shall *agree* on earth as touching any thing that they shall ask, it shall be done for them of my Father which is in heaven."

---

Evil thoughts are worse enemies than lions and tigers; for we can get out of the way of wild beasts, but bad thoughts win their way every where. The cup that is full will hold no more. Keep your heads and hearts full of good thoughts, that bad thoughts may not find room.

Conversation. — The art of conversation consists in the exercise of two fine qualities. You must originate, and you must sympathize, — you must possess at the same time the habit of communicating and listening. The union is rare but irresistible.

## THE BIBLE.

A WRITER has said, "The Holy Scriptures are a bed of the goodliest pearls, and the deeper we dive into the sea of divine revelation, the larger, more beautiful, and more costly they are. They are a mine of the purest gold, and the most soul-enriching treasure. The book of God is a casket of the rarest and richest gems, which bespangle the soul of the wearer, rendering it most brilliant in the eyes of Christ — even like a bride adorned with her jewels. In a word, as the Song of Solomon is the 'Song of songs,' and as the Lord Jesus is the 'King of kings,' so the Bible is the 'Book of books.'"

> The Bible, the Bible, more precious than gold,
> What wonders on wonders its pages unfold!
> 'Tis the word of Jehovah, all blessèd and pure;
> Its truths shall forever and ever endure.
>
> The Bible, — it shows us the Lord on his throne,
> Creator, Upholder, Redeemer, alone;

Eternal, unchangeable, dwelling in light,
His ways are eternally holy and right.


The Bible, — it shows us how vile we have been,
How we have polluted our nature by sin;
How we dared against God and his Son to rebel,
And how we deserve to be cast down to hell.


The Bible, — it points to a Saviour who died;
To Christ our Redeemer, for us crucified;
His blood is most precious, for us it was spilt;
'Tis always sufficient to cleanse us from guilt.


The Bible, — it speaks of the Spirit divine;
With light and with glory the Spirit doth shine
In the souls of all Christians, to guide them aright,
To lead them to Jesus, the Source of all light.


The Bible, — a lamp 'tis to light up our way,
To show us most clearly the truth day by day;
O, may we cling to it, as to us it is given,
That we may at last dwell with Jesus in heaven.


The Bible, — it points to a kingdom of love
Reserved in the mansions of heaven above;
There dwell saints and angels, a glorious throng,
Praising God and the Lamb evermore in their song.

May we the blest Bible peruse more and more;
The God of the Bible, O may we adore;
Then at last we shall meet with the holy on high,
Where pleasures ne'er fade, and where joys never die.

---

THE BIBLE IN TURKEY. — The British and American agents for the diffusion of the Word of God at Constantinople, have great success in their work. French and English officers encourage the enterprise. In a single month, two thousand seven hundred and fifty Italian Testaments were distributed among the Sardinian troops, two thousand French Testaments among the Savoyards, one hundred and sixty to the English, and a large number to the Russian prisoners. The Mohammedans, in considerable numbers, are purchasing the Bible. Several Turks, as colporteurs, are selling it.

IT is better to have a good conscience and be censured, than to have a bad one and be flattered.

## THE OLD FAMILY BIBLE.

How painfully pleasing the fond recollection
    Of youthful emotion and innocent joy,
When blessed with parental advice and affection,
    Surrounded with mercies, with peace from on high!
I still view the chair of my sire and my mother,
    The seats of their offspring as ranged on each hand,
And that richest book which excels every other,
    That family Bible which lay on the stand:
The old-fashioned Bible, the dear, blesséd Bible,
    The family Bible that lay on the stand.

That Bible, the volume of God's inspiration,
    At morn and at even could yield us delight;
The prayer of our sire was a sweet invocation
    For mercy by day and safety through night.
Our hymns of thanksgiving with harmony swelling,
    All warm from the heart of a family band,
Half raised us from earth to that rapturous dwelling
    Described in the Bible that lay on the stand:
The old-fashioned Bible, the dear, blesséd Bible,
    The family Bible that lay on the stand.

Ye scenes of tranquillity, long have we parted,
    My hopes almost gone and my parents no more;
In sorrow and sadness I live broken-hearted,
    And wander unknown on a far-distant shore.

Yet how can I doubt a dear Saviour's protection ;
   Forgetful of gifts from his bountiful hand ;
O, let me with patience receive his correction,
   And think of the Bible that lay on the stand :
The old-fashioned Bible, the dear, blesséd Bible,
   The family Bible that lay on the stand.

---

BELIEVE. — Dr. Johnson could not find the primary meaning, nor the origin of the word *believe*. It was formed from the Gothic *Belifian*, which is something by which a person lives. When a man believes any thing, he adapts his life to it. Hence the great significance of this word. When a man professes to believe Christianity, and fails to conform his life to it, he thereby shows that he does not believe what he professes. There are many such persons, to whom Plato's use of the word *opinion* may be correctly applied. Plato said that "opinion is the half-way house between ignorance and knowledge ;" and a great many opinions take their final lounge in the dominion of ignorance.

## THE BIBLE AND ITS INFLUENCE.

ALL Scripture is given by inspiration of God; and is profitable for doctrine, for reproof, for correction, for instruction in righteousness. — 2 *Tim.* iii. 16.

>     Hast thou ever heard
> Of such a book? The author, God himself;
> The subject, God and man, salvation, life
> And death, — eternal life — eternal death.
> · *Pollok.*

The Bible is a window in this prison of hope, through which we look into eternity. — *Dwight.*

> O! 'tis pleasant, 'tis reviving,
>   To our hearts, to hear each day,
> Joyful news from far arriving,
>   How the Gospel wins its way!
>     Those enlightening,
>   Who in death and darkness lay.
> *Kelly.*

The word of God must be nearer to us than our friends; dearer to us than our lives; sweeter to us than our liberty, and pleasanter to us than all earthly comforts. — *J. Mason.*

><br>O ! let thy word of grace
> My warmest thoughts employ;
> Be this, through all my following days,
> My treasure and my joy.      *Fawcett.*

In studying the word of God, digest it under these two heads: either as removing some obstructions that keep God and thee asunder, or as supplying some uniting power to bring God and thee together. — *Cecil.*

> Within this ample volume lies
> The mystery of mysteries;
> Happiest they, of human race,
> To whom their God has given grace,
> To read, to fear, to hope, to pray,
> To lift the latch, to force the way;
> And better had they ne'er been born,
> That read to doubt, or read to scorn.
>                 *Sir Walter Scott.*

We account the Scriptures of God to be the most sublime philosophy. — *Sir Isaac Newton.*

> What glory gilds the sacred page!
> Majestic like the sun;
> It gives a light to every age,
> It gives, but borrows none. *Cowper.*

The Scriptures contain, independently of a divine origin, more true sublimity, more exquisite beauty, purer morality, more important history, and finer strains both of poetry and eloquence, than could be collected within the same compass from all other books that were ever composed in any age or in any idiom. — *Sir W. Jones.*

Thy word have I hid in my heart, that I might not sin against thee. — *Psalm* cxix. 11.

## WHY I ATTEND CHURCH ON RAINY SABBATHS.

1. Because God has blessed the Sabbath day and hallowed it, making no exceptions for rainy Sabbaths.

2. Because I expect *my minister* to be there; I should be surprised if *he* were to stay at home for the weather.

3. Because, if his hands fall through weakness, I shall have great reason to blame myself, unless I sustain him by my prayers and by my presence.

4. Because, by staying away, I may lose the sermon that would have done me great good, and the prayers which bring God's blessing.

5. Because my presence is more needed on Sabbaths when there are few, than on those days when the church is crowded.

6. Because, whatever station I hold in the church, my example must influence others: if I stay away, why may not they?

7. Because, on my important business, bad weather does not keep me at home; and church attendance is, in God's sight, very important. (See Heb. x. 25.)

8. Because, among the crowds of pleasure-seekers, I see that no bad weather keeps the delicate female from the ball, the party, or the concert.

9. Because, among other blessings, such weather will show me on what foundation my faith is built. It will prove how much I love Christ: true love rarely fails to meet an appointment.

10. Because those who stay from church because it is too warm, or too cold, or too rainy, frequently absent themselves on fair Sabbaths.

11. Because, though my excuses satisfy myself, they still must undergo God's scrutiny; and they must be well grounded to bear that. (Luke xiv. 18.)

12. Because there is a *special* promise that where two or three meet together in God's name, he will be in the midst of them.

13. Because an avoidable absence from church is an infallible evidence of spiritual decay. Disciples first follow Christ at a distance, and then, like Peter, do not know him.

14. Because my faith is to be known by my self-denying Christian life, and not by the rise or fall of the thermometer.

15. Because such yielding to surmountable difficulties prepares for yielding to those merely imaginary, until thousands never enter a church, and yet think they have good reasons for such neglect.

16. Because, by a suitable arrangement on Saturday, I shall be able to attend church without exhaustion; otherwise my late work on Saturday night will be as great a sin as though I worked on the Sabbath itself.

17. Because I know not how many more Sabbaths God may give me; and it would be a poor preparation for my first Sabbath in heaven to have slighted my last Sabbath on earth.

## MEDICINE FOR THE DISCONSOLATE.

A CLERGYMAN called on a rich parishioner and found him sad. "Sir, I feel as though God and all mankind had forsaken me."

"I think I can prescribe for you a remedy. Go and relieve some poor family in distress."

He found it was the medicine he needed, for while we are doing good to others we forget our own troubles, and we receive a heavenly frame of mind which fits and prepares us for every day's duty. "Do good unto all men as you have opportunity." A child of seven years says, "Mother, I am a going to be always happy, for I am a going to forget myself, and try to make others happy." This is the spirit in which we should live.

Speak evil of no man, "for the measure we mete to others shall be measured to us again." God's eye is upon us; he knows it all. Take no man's word for the Bible. "Search it as for your life, for out of it are the issues of eternal life." Cherish pure thoughts, and make them known by word or writing. Let the Bible be your principal reading.

---

PROFANITY. — The famous Dr. Johnson never suffered an oath to go unrebuked in his presence. When a libertine, but a man of some note, was once talking before him, and interlarding his stories with oaths, Johnson said, " Sir, all this swearing will do nothing for our story; I beg you will not swear." The narrator went on a swearing. Johnson said, " I must again entreat you not to swear." The gentleman swore again, and Johnson indignantly quitted the room.

EMBLEM OF FRIENDSHIP. — Trees with double flowers are too often the emblem of friendship — there is plenty of blossoms, but no fruit

## ADULTERATED LIQUORS.

Dr. Hiram Cox, the Cincinnati inspector, has published many deeply interesting facts of his experience in testing liquors sold in that city. In seven hundred inspections of stores and lots of liquor of every variety, he found that ninety per cent. were impregnated with the most pernicious and poisonous ingredients. Nineteen young men, all sons of respectable citizens, were killed outright by only three months' drinking of these poisoned liquors. Many older men, who were only moderate drinkers, died within the same period of the delirium tremens, brought on in one quarter the time usual, even with confirmed drunkards, by drinking the same poison. Of four hundred insane patients, he found that two thirds had lost their reason from the same cause. Many of them were boys under age. One boy of seventeen was made insane by the poison from being drunk only once. Seeing two men drinking in a grog-shop, and that the whiskey was so strong that it actually caused tears to flow from the eyes of one of them, the doctor obtained some of it and applied the tests. He found it to contain only seventeen per cent. of alcohol, when it should have had forty, and that the difference was supplied by sulphuric acid, red pepper, caustic, potassa, and strychnine. A pint of this liquor contained enough poison to kill the strongest man. The man who had manufactured it had grown wealthy by producing it.

---

TEARS soften the heart and produce repentance. A father correcting his son with a rod, seeing he did not yield, he wept aloud. Father, I cannot endure your tears. I acknowledge my wrong, and ask your forgiveness. The rod hardens the heart, tears soften. Let a father take his wayward son into a retired room, with penitent tears for his own sins. "Come, let us reason together," saith the Bible.

## SCENE IN A GROG-SHOP.

A WELL-KNOWN colporteur in a Southern city, who labors faithfully among all classes, thus graphically sketches a scene in which he was an actor. "Went into a drinking-house where were thirteen men. 'Well, gentlemen, any books for you this morning?' 'No,' was the reply; 'I'll buy no books from a man that won't drink with us.' 'Why, gentlemen,' said I, 'there is not a man here but would be as sorry to see me drink, as to see me rode on a rail.' 'That's a fact, old gentleman; I would not sell you a glass of liquor for five dollars, no, not for ten dollars, for I believe you are trying to do good; and if you have any good book there that you think I need, I'll buy it. Come, men,' said he, 'come up, and let's buy the whole lot, and help along.' Here in the grog-shop, among decanters, and demijohns, and barrels, I sold an armful of books, gave each man a temperance tract, and left all in good humor."

## A VISIT TO THE TOMBS, COURT SQUARE.

From a gentleman that accompanied Father Mason to the Tombs, we gather the following. On his way to the chapel prayer-meeting he meets the Rev. Mr. Mason.

"Will you go to the prayer-meeting with me?"

"Sir, I would gladly go with you, but at this hour every morning I go to the Tombs to encourage the prisoners to lead a better life. Please go with me."

In coming up to the first tomb, occupied by a woman about thirty, we hear the following: —

"What are you here for?"

"I have been taking a drop."

"I guess you have, a good many. Plead guilty; perhaps they will let you off with a fine."

In the next tomb, we found it occupied by two girls about twenty.

"What are you here for?"

"We have been taking a little too much."

"I guess you have been taking a good deal too much. Plead guilty, and when you get home, do you take off those turbans, and never wear them again."

We next came to a tomb occupied by a man about thirty-five.

"What are you here for?"

"I got a little tight. Can you speak a word for me?"

"Yours is a doubtful case, you had better plead guilty."

Passing several tombs in this way, we soon came to one occupied by five boys, ranging from six to nine.

"What are you here for?"

"We have been breaking into a building and stealing."

If any of their mothers read this, let their first business be to find a Sabbath-school teacher. The mission that this apostle started in North Street still prospers. He has gone to his rest, to reap his reward. May God send another to make his place good.

OR, THE WAY TO DO GOOD. 315

These criminals work for the government nearly half of their time without pay. Can they afford it? Is it not too heavy a tax for them? We spend thousands of dollars in punishing crime, swelling our tax bills to an enormous size, and what are we doing to prevent crime? If we do not want our city to become as Sodom, we must do something soon. A judge asked a criminal, who had been to the House of Correction two or three times, why he could not learn to keep away. "I cannot resist the temptation of the liquor bottles I see in the windows. Take away the liquor shops and I shall be all right." Let there be a thorough organized missionary enterprise. You can conquer a man with kindness, but you cannot by driving. Furnish your missionaries with five hundred New Testaments. Place in each a circular, enclose each Testament in a wrapper, with the shopkeeper's address. Offer a premium for the best circular, showing a mother's tears over her starving children and drunken husband. And the liquor shop, the parent of all crime, closing with this promise, — Good business shall be furnished to all that will give up their shop." As the missionary presents the Testament to the proprietor, let him set forth the object of his mission. Small Testaments can be bought for six or eight cents. Perhaps the Bible Society will make us a donation. A few dollars spent in this way is better than thousands in punishing crime.

Some of these shopkeepers are well-educated young men from the best of families. All they want, is a kind hand, and they will return, as the prodigal returned. Let this mission be started forthwith. Without God's blessing it will amount to nothing. I have perfect faith in prayer. Let the whole church of Christ, set apart a week for this object. And may the Great Head of the Church crown this mission with his blessing.

## INCREASE OF CRIME, AND ITS REMEDY.

Sooner or later the public mind will be more effectually turned to this subject. Criminals, both imported and of native growth, are fearfully increasing among us. If there were no emigrations of foreigners hither, there are in the quickened action of all causes that form character, whether good or bad, reasons why we should expect that the more depraved among our native population would more rapidly advance in crimes against society than formerly. Then, in addition to this source of increase, the jails and poor-houses of Europe are discharging their contents among us to such an extent that only a small fraction of the tenants of our prisons are of American birth. Speaking of the growth of crime in New York, the Journal of Commerce says, —

" We have in this city nine cases of murder and attempts to kill, on hand. Two men have recently been executed, and two more are to share the same fate. Two policemen have recently been killed, and several more are dangerously wounded. The knife is used frequently and fearfully. Rowdyism is increasing all over the city. Look at the numerous gambling houses, brothels, grog-shops, and other hot-beds of vice. What is to be done? What can be done? The world is vomiting its tens of thousands upon us every year, and too many of them come surcharged with infidelity or superstition, and not a few are adepts in crime."

"What is to be done?" is the question. No radical changes in our criminal laws will reach the case. And little more can be hoped from a more rigid and severe system of administering the laws. Judge Parsons, of Pennsylvania, who has had much experience in the administration of criminal laws, says,—

"If the city and county of Philadelphia could appropriate the sum of fifty thousand dollars annually for five years for missionary purposes, more than that amount would be saved to the people in the sustenance of paupers, the administration of law, and the pay of police officers."

This suggests the nature of the effectual remedy, though under an impossible supposition of its being applied by the civil government. It accords with the genius of our institutions to bring religious and moral influence to bear only through voluntary organizations. And if we were to depart from this principle, and establish a State religion, we should, as all experience proves, thereby corrupt religion, and diminish instead of increasing its reforming powers.

It comes, then, to this, that there is a true and effectual remedy; but it is one which civil officers, as such, cannot use — one whose expense cannot be borne from the State treasury. It is now in use to a limited but inadequate extent, because a great portion of those who have lives and property to be protected stand wholly aloof from our Christian institutions. And many who bear some connection with them, fail of contributing their share to a thorough evangelizing of the masses around them. Now the course of events is forcing upon our attention the necessity of some adequate means of home evangelizing — of bringing the masses of the people, especially in our own cities and larger towns, under the influence of the gospel. God is driving us into a corner, where we shall be compelled to do it, as our only means of escape from destruction. And it is time, not for the church only, but for all who desire protection of life and property under wholesome laws, to consider what is their interest and duty to do in the premises.

God has put into our hands an instrument by which the people can be made obedient to law, and crimes be diminished. The responsibility as to its use rests with individuals, and not with civil authorities. It cannot be applied by constables paid by the city, but by ministers of the gospel and their helpers, fed by voluntary means. This is a fact which especially deserves the consideration of men of wealth

in our cities. They consent to be heavily
taxed to pay the police expenses of the city, the
costs of criminal prosecution, and the support
of pauperism, resulting from vice and crime,
and little think that a liberal support of evangelizing agencies would save them a great
share of this taxation.

The great obstacle to a proper appreciation
of this subject by such men, is, that having
little experience of the gospel themselves, they
have little faith in it. They do not readily
realize the fitness of the instrument to the
result. This fact raises the question, whether
some special means might not be used with
profit, to produce a broader public conviction
that the gospel is the power of God to do this
work, and induce many who have been indifferent to it, to give a generous support to our
systems of home evangelizing. Besides appeal-
ing to the public through the ordinary channels for the support of missions, home and
foreign, for the support of Bible societies and
tract societies and their colporteurs, might not

an effective appeal be made out on general grounds, through public conventions and the press, to this class of people, compelling them to see that their security of life and property, and their share in the public safety, require their coöperation in home evangelizing, — not through this or that agency or sect, but through some agency, leaving each to choose for himself. The thing to be demonstrated, to the conviction of the hitherto indifferent, is that the application of gospel power can and will do this work and that nothing else will. The effectual tending of this simple truth to all who have an interest in the prevention of crime, would become a moral revolution. Who have a high vantage ground from which to inculcate it — in a world of facts that are incontrovertible, and in the strong interest which all have in finding a remedy. Let the energies of our most powerful minds be employed, to set in array these facts and arguments addressed to the interest of individuals. Let there be a concentration of mental power upon this single theme, and much might be done. But, be it this or that, something must be done over and above any thing now in progress. For crime, in its worst forms, is increasing out of all proportion to what is done to prevent it.

---

TRUE TO HIS PLEDGE. — Mr. J. W. Goodrich, of Worcester, through whose efforts John B. Gough was induced to give up drinking, recently died. Previous to his death he insisted on being removed from the place where he was sick, because, when insensible and supposed to be dying, rum was administered to him. "Be sure and keep the pledge," were among his last words to one whom he had been the means of reforming.

RICHES do not so often produce criminals as incite accusers.

## THE LITTLE ONES AT PRAYER.

A little child knelt near the broken lattice. Casting a glance at the sleeping form of her father, she clasped her wan hands and murmured, —

"O God, make father leave his evil ways; make him my own dear father once again! Make mother's sad looks go away, and make her old smile come back; but thy way will be done."

Just then the mother entered the room; and taking her husband by the arm, she said, —

"Hearken to Minnie; she is praying."

"O God, make father love me, as once he did; and make him forsake his bad ways," murmured the little one again.

"O Paul — husband!" cried the mother; "by our past joys and sorrows, by our marriage vows, our wedded love, blight not the life of our little one! O, let us all be happy again!"

The conscience-stricken man bowed his head and wept. Then, clasping his hands, he said, —

"With God's help, you will never be made to sorrow on my account again."

And he kept his vow.

---

OBSERVANCE OF THE SABBATH. — The sheriff of London repeats an old maxim of a Puritan divine, that "if the Sabbath is well hemmed, it will not ravel out during all the week." He has learned from the confessions of most of the prisoners, that their crimes originated in Sabbath-breaking.

THIN SHOES. — A tombstone somewhere in New Jersey bears the following significant epitaph : "Died of thin shoes, January, 1839." If the truth were always spoken, there would be many epitaphs of that description.

## FAITH IN GOD.

Have faith in God. Faith will be staggered even by loose stones in the way, if we look Manward; if we look Godward, faith will not be staggered by inaccessible mountains stretching across and obstructing apparently our onward progress. "Go forward," is the voice from heaven; and faith obeying, finds the mountains before it as flat as plains. "God with us," is the watchward of our warfare, the secret of our strength, the security of our triumph. "If thou canst believe, all things are possible to him that believeth." How strong faith is when we are just fresh from the fountain of redeeming love! A good conscience, and then faith will do all things, for it is in its very nature such as to let God work all; we may say that it is the most active when it is most passive, and that it wearies least when it does most work.

## THE STATE OF PROBATION.

The seed we sow in the ground has its successive stages of beauty and utility — " first the blade, then the ear, after that the full corn in the ear ; " and, having thus attained the limit of its existence, it dies, to live again a hundredfold. True it is that the world changes less than its inhabitants ; still the truths of nature aid us in understanding those higher revelations of grace which instruct us that our present state is one of probation, and far, very far, from being that in which human nature can attain its noblest dignity and happiness — a state of progression introductory to a holier and a better one, of unchangeable nature and endless duration. Woe to them who live as if earth were home! Woe to them who live as if Christ had never died for them, risen again for them, and ascended into heaven to prepare a place for them forever.

## ETERNITY.

ETERNITY has no gray hairs. The flowers fade, the heart withers, man grows old and dies; the world lies down in the sepulchre of ages, but Time writes no wrinkles on Eternity. Eternity! Stupendous thought! The ever-present, unborn, undecaying and undying, the endless chain, compassing the life of God; the golden thread, entwining the destinies of the universe. Earth has its beauties, but time shrouds them for the grave; its honors are but the sunshine of an hour; its palaces, they are but the gilded sepulchres; its pleasures, they are but as bursting bubbles. Not so in the untried bourn. In the dwelling of the Almighty can come no footsteps of decay.

---

NATURAL LAW. — Every vice has its penalty. The lazy must expect to be poor; the intemperate to be diseased; the luxurious to die young.

## DIVINITY OF CHRIST.

Two gentlemen were engaged in a discussion on the Divinity of Christ. One of them, who argued against it, said, 'If it were true, it certainly would have been expressed in more clear and unequivocal terms." "Well" said the other, "admitting that you believed it, were authorized to teach it, and allowed to use your own language, how would you express the doctrine, to make it satisfactory and indubitable?" "I would say," replied the first, "that Jesus Christ is the *true God!*" "You are happy," rejoined the other, "in the choice of your words, for you have happened to hit upon the very words of inspiration. St. John, speaking of Christ, says, 'This is *the true God*, and eternal life!'" — John v. 20.

---

He who can take advice is superior to him who gives it.

## EXPERIENCE.

GREAT is the difference between the experimental reality of human life and that beauteous picture of earthly bliss which the young and buoyant heart is wont to paint. Ripened experience and matured judgment go far to modify the hasty and crude decisions of the untutored and untried imagination. In the morning of life the future appears bright, and the prospect altogether lovely; but more mature age, without extinguishing this joyous feeling, chastens and subdues it, enables it to find a more substantial basis, teaches it to cling more to that which is really and intrinsically good, and to be guided more by the sound deductions of wisdom than by external fascinations, which fade away whilst we admire them, and perish in using them.

## FROM LAVATER.

ALL that pertains to humanity is, for us, a family affair. Thou art *man;* and all else which is man is as a branch of the same tree, a limb of the same body. O man! rejoice in the existence of all which rejoices to exist, and learn to endure all which God allows. The existence of one man cannot render that of another superfluous, and no man can replace another.

Be faithful in the smallest matters. Fix thy attention upon that which thou dost, as though thou hadst but that alone to do. He who has acted well in the present moment, has accomplished a good action for all eternity. Simplify all things in acting, in enjoying, in suffering. Give thy heart to Him who governs hearts. Be just and exact in the least details. Hope in the future, know how to wait, know how to enjoy all, and learn to do without all.

## A FRAGMENT FROM ANDREW FULLER.

"As to myself, I feel a good deal dejected at times, thinking I shall never be of much use. My writing and preaching seem to want something, and God withholds his blessing from me. I was thinking this week on John xv. 8. *Fruit* is more than regularity of conduct or respectability of character. We may be kept from God-dishonoring crimes, and yet be 'unprofitable servants.' *Much* fruit is necessary to do honor to a gardener. Here and there a berry may ascertain the nature of a plant or tree, but it is the *loaded branch* that honors him that planted it. I have been thinking also on Psalm xcii. 'Fruits in old age.' I am turned of fifty-four. I want to find the cluster mentioned in Romans v. — 'Patience — Experience — Hope!'"

---

THE path of duty is the only path of safety.

## TWO CLASSES OF CHRISTIANS.

THERE are two classes of Christians: those who live chiefly by emotion, and those who live chiefly by faith. The first class, those who live chiefly by emotion, remind one of ships, that move by the outward impulse of winds operating upon sails. They are often at a dead calm, often out of their course, and sometimes driven back. And it is only when the winds are fair and powerful that they move onward with rapidity. The other class, those who live chiefly by faith, remind one of the magnificent steamers which cross the Atlantic, which are moved by an interior and permanent principle, and which, setting at defiance all ordinary obstacles, advance steadily and swiftly to the destination, through calm and storm, through cloud and sunshine.

---

LUXURY. — The greatest luxury is doing good. It is the peculiar food of the mind. No fleshly banquet can equal it.

## "MY LIFE HAS BEEN A FAILURE."

So said a capitalist in this country worth his several millions, on being asked why he did not have a biography of his life written. What an answer, and what a sad truth, to be made and considered by one who has spent a whole life in amassing wealth, and now, with trembling limbs, stepping into the grave, the startling truth, quite to late, it is to be feared, flashes across his mind, *that his life had been a failure* — its great object, and the only one worthy the attention of an immortal being, having been entirely overlooked and neglected! What more than such a thought need occupy a sane mind, to fill and keep it full of unutterable anguish? Life a failure! Probation squandered — ending! the soul lost!

Reader, whoever you may be, poor or rich, did you ever ask yourself whether *your* life also has not been a failure? — whether you are living merely for this world? laying up the treasures which cannot avail yourself in your time of greatest need? Will you go to the judgment with the awful truth sounding in your ears, that *your* life has been a failure? If you would not, mend that life — mend it to-day; to-morrow is not yours. Put off no longer a work so important, involving your all, and one which should have been done the first day of your accountability.

---

I CALLED last evening to see a friend, who, with his family, has not, until very recently, attended church for five years past.

It was stated that some thirty or forty inquirers were in the vestry after sermon.

A brother requested prayers for the youngest son of a family of five children. All the others have been brought into the kingdom, — two sisters about six weeks since. The one for whom prayers were requested, was last evening in a state of deep anxiety for the salvation of his soul.

## WHAT PLEASES GOD WILL PLEASE ME.

We were much impressed in reading, a few days since, this declaration of a deeply afflicted Christian, a great sufferer under the hand of God, and who in a short time was carried to the grave. Yet he was happy — very happy — in thus having his will swallowed up in that of his heavenly Father. What a burden of vexation and anxious sorrow will this spirit of holy resignation to the divine will lift from the soul! and how will it sweeten not only mercies, but even sharp affliction, thus to receive all as the wise and holy dispensations of Him whose will is always supremely right and good, and therefore just what ought to occur in all circumstances of toil, pain and trial! "Even so, Father, for it seemeth good in thy sight."

## WORTHY OF RESPECT.

He alone is worthy of respect, who is of use to himself and others, and who labors to control his self-will. Each man has a fortune in his hands, as the artist has a piece of rude matter, which he is to fashion to a certain shape. But the art of living rightly is like all arts; the capacity is born with us; it must be learned and practised with incessant care.

---

Rise up in the name and strength of God, and set thyself in earnest to thy duty; honestly study to know and do the will of God; take heed of defiling thy conscience with any known or wilful sin; call upon God for his grace, by constant and daily prayer; and in this way of well-doing, commit thy soul to the goodness and mercy of God in Christ Jesus; and whilst thou do so, be assured that thou art safe, and canst never miscarry.

## ANECDOTE OF DANIEL WEBSTER.

It is related of Mr. Webster, that while pacing the halls of Marshfield he sought repose from disturbing agitations of threatened trouble with Great Britain in chanting to himself those lines that have become immortal in our Christian worship: —

> "Eternity, with all its years,
>   Stands present to thy view:
> To thee there's nothing old appears,
>   Great God, there's nothing new.
>
> "Our lives through various scenes are passed,
>   And vexed with trifling cares,
> While thine eternal thoughts move on,
>   Thine undisturbed affairs."

How to divide the minutes of life profitably seems the thing to be found out; and what degree of attention to bestow on one object, and what on another, the question to be decided.

## BE SOCIAL.

How different would be the aspect of human society if all persons would throw aside some of the reserve they have, and be more open, frank, and sociable than they are now. In most instances now, when strangers meet, there is a coldness and reserve which dampens the flow of good feeling, and freezes up the affections of the heart. How we have been pained to see individuals thrown into each other's presence when the fountains of the heart were locked up, and no disposition manifested to let them loose by social conversation. A single word, well-timed and fitly spoken under such circumstances, would do more to relieve individuals of their embarrassment than any thing else. And why should not every body so far forget conventional forms as to be sociable to strangers when thrown into their presence? Americans are wanting in this respect.

## IN THE GARDEN.

Every man that can afford it — and we may add, every woman too — should have a garden. The merchant who busies himself all day in his counting-room; the tailor who toils from morning till night on his bench; the editor who writes and clips, and clips and writes, till the universe seems to him no more than a dry, rustling newspaper; the clergyman who pores over his theology till the juice of nature dies out of it and out of his flesh; the sedentary females shortening their respiration and their lives over their interminable sewing; all should have some such refreshing outdoor interest for evening and morning recreation.

There is something here, among these stalks, and blossoms, and vines, that gives breath to the sick, strength to the weak, rest to the weary, and happiness to the discontented. You bury your troubles under the rich soil you turn over with your spade. You dig up cares with the weeds. You train up sweet sentiments and gentle thoughts with the fragrant pea-vines and rose bushes. The opening of a morning-glory symbolizes the expanding beauty of your soul. The rotund melons, swelling and swelling to ripeness, the homely potato-top, the tassels and silk of the corn, or the heliotropes, foxgloves, pinks, sweet-williams, — all have something friendly and soothing to say to you, when you come home disappointed and grieved, from your transactions in the world.

There is something in these subtle influences which we do not always appreciate, but which is none the less real and beneficial. The manual labor which reinvigorates the blood, brings back color and appetite, and restores the youthful joy of living, is not more certainly effective than the magnetism of the earth, the wholesome smell, the sight of greenness and growth, and the mild, silent, and subduing lessons of the plants.

## CHEERFULNESS.

Try for a single day, I beseech you, to preserve yourself in an easy and cheerful frame of mind. Be, for one day, instead of a fire-worshipper of passion and hell, the sun-worshipper of clear self-possession; and compare the day in which you have rooted out the weed of dissatisfaction with that on which you have allowed it to grow up, and you will find your heart open to every good motive, your life strengthened, and your breast armed with a panoply against every trick of fate. Truly you will wonder at your own improvement.

---

"I just now met Mr. Bushe on the North Parade, who told me there was very bad news; but I did not ask about it, and *I dare not open a paper on the Lord's day*," said Wilberforce. Was that being too strict? No. "Them that honor me, I will honor."

## THE LIFE-PRESERVER.

Commencing a long journey, which was to take me upon most of our western lakes and rivers, I took the precaution to provide myself with a life-preserver of the best construction. My reasons for doing this were these. I had always felt great confidence in these simple instruments. They are constructed on principles perfectly philosophical. Several individuals from the circle of my own acquaintance had been saved by them when in imminent peril. The expense of the article was very trifling. It was not at all in the way. So far from this, I found it a positive convenience, as a cushion by day and a pillow by night.

My custom was, every night before retiring to sleep, to examine my life-preserver, and see that it was where I could place my hand upon it in an instant; and often, when the winds blew, and the waves dashed against the boat, I felt a sense of security in the possession of that which, with the blessing of God, might preserve me in an emergency; and this of itself amply repaid me for my purchase.

Soon after entering the Mississippi River, we were not a little agitated by an accident which befell the boat. The night was dark and tempestuous, and the "Father of waters" angry and frightful. The passengers sprung from their births, and rushed together into the main saloon. The accident proved to be of small consequence, and the alarm very soon subsided.

Returning to my state-room with this incident fresh in mind, I fell into a sort of waking dream. I thought I was on one of our inland seas, in a violent tempest. Our vessel, dismasted and disabled, was rapidly driving on a lee shore. Death, in one of its most frightful forms, was staring us in the face, for the captain was heard to say, "We are all gone for this world." The passengers were evidently making ready for the last struggle. And now I observed, for the first time, that some, amid the general consternation, seemed perfectly calm and composed. They were very solemn, but gave no sign of fear. On looking again, I saw that they were provided with life-preservers, large and strong, of the very best kind. These they had already attached to their persons; and feeling the utmost confidence in this means of preservation, they were quietly waiting the issue. An emotion of joy was depicted on their countenances, as if they were thanking God that they had secured, in good season, what was now of great price.

But how shall I describe the terrors and dismay of the other passengers, as they passed to and fro before my eye. Very few had any hope of reaching the shore. Their faces were pale, and they wrung their hands in despair.

"What a fool I was," said one, "that I did not buy a life-preserver before I left home! *I always meant to do it.* They were exposed for sale right before my eye every day. My friends entreated me to procure one, and I promised that I would. I thought I could obtain one at any time. *But I put it off, and now it is too late.*"

"*I did not believe there was any danger,*" said another. "I have passed over these lakes many times, and never saw such a storm before. 'Tis true, I was warned that come they would, in an hour when I looked not for them; but as I had passed safely without a life-preserver before, *I concluded to run the risk again.*"

Another I observed hastening to his trunk, and returning instantly with the case of a life-preserver in his hand, but an expression of blank despair on his countenance. The article had once been good, but he *had not taken care of it*. He had thrown it loosely among his effects, and it had been punctured by a pin. It was now a mockery of his woe. He tried to mend it, but this was impossible. There was not time for this.

Another produced, with great joy, what seemed an excellent life-preserver, but when he proceeded to adjust it, he found that he had been cheated. *It was a counterfeit article.* He did not procure it at the right place. *To all appearance* it was sound. It would retain its shape and buoyancy for a while, but would-not *bear the pressure of a man's whole weight.* It would answer very well for a few minutes in smooth water, but *could not be relied on in an emergency.* He had never examined it before; and now, in the hour of need, found it utterly worthless.

At length my eye was arrested by a young man who had been notorious throughout the voyage for his gayety and frivolity. On one occasion, during a pleasant day, he had made sport of those who had wisely prepared for the time of peril. He pronounced their forethought a waste of money. And now I saw him addressing a gentleman whom he had previously ridiculed, and in a subdued and anxious manner inquiring whether his life-preserver was not capable of saving them both. The man replied that he would most gladly extend any help in his power, but it was *made only for one person,* and was not warranted to sustain more.

Reader, THERE IS A HOPE WHICH IS AS AN ANCHOR TO THE SOUL, BOTH SURE AND STEADFAST. The ground on which it rests is the mercy of God, through our Lord Jesus Christ. The time is coming when you *will certainly need it.* Life may now be like a smooth and sunny sea, but very soon you will be amid the swellings of Jordan.

A good hope in Christ *is certain to save.* Never did one perish who possessed it. It was never known to disappoint in the time of need. Millions have been saved by it; and God has promised that it shall never make ashamed. Is it not wise for you to obtain it?

To say the least, *it can do you no harm*, should there be no judgment nor retribution. It cannot encumber you during your lifetime. It is worth every thing, even in prosperous days, and beneath cloudless skies. The sense of security which religion creates is of great price. To know that, whatever may happen, you are safe; to be confident that " neither life nor death, things present nor things to come, nor height, nor depth, nor any other creature, is able to separate us from the love of God which is in Christ Jesus our Lord:" is it not worth more than all silver and gold?

Moreover, this hope *may easily be obtained.* It is " set before you." It is pressed upon your acceptance. Because of this, do not say that you can obtain it at any time. For this is not true. There is no time to forge and bend an anchor when the storm is raging. If you postpone repentance too long, disappointment and destruction will overtake you *without* remedy. Do not delay the pursuit of religion; Seek it first of all. Pious friends entreat you to seek it now. The experience of those who have delayed too long, and died " without hope," warns you to be wise in season.

Be careful that your *hope is of the right kind.* There is a hope which perisheth when God taketh away the soul. There are false spirits, false religions, false hopes, and counterfeit graces. Examine well the hope which is in you. Be sure that it rests on the right foundation, Jesus Christ being the chief corner-stone.

If you have found hope in Christ, *take care of your hope.* Protect it from injury; watch it; keep it with *all diligence.* And as you cannot tell the day nor the hour when the Son of man cometh, be always ready. Let your light be trimmed and burning, as men that wait for their Lord. Death can never be unexpected, if you are always anticipating it; never sudden, if you are always prepared for it.

Remember, that religion is a concern between your own soul and God. The conduct of others is no excuse for you. "He that is wise, is wise for himself; and he that scorneth, he alone must bear it." Soon, very soon the hour of trial will come. The winds will blow, the rain fall, and the floods come, and the great storm beat against your house. You must go down into the river of death alone. Friends cannot go with you; they cannot help you. But "he that believeth in Jesus is safe," even when the waves and billows go over his soul.

The arm of the Redeemer will keep you from sinking; and amidst the pains and mysteries of dying you may lift up your head and say, "Thou wilt keep him in perfect peace whose mind is stayed on thee;" and a voice from heaven shall answer, "Fear not: when thou passest through the waters, I will be with thee; and through the rivers; they shall not overflow thee;" and, borne along by the "everlasting arms" which are beneath you, you shall reach in safety that peaceful shore where the grateful spirit shall rest with God.

---

A REMEDY WORTH TRYING. — One church-member told another, who was complaining of the constant call for donations, that he used to be annoyed, until he found that his trouble arose from teasing his mind in making excuses why he should not give. Since then he had adopted the plan of giving freely, and he found not only that he felt much better, but that the annoyance had ceased.

## DOUBT FROM INACTIVITY.

We cannot give the philosophy of it, but this is the fact: Christians who have nothing to do but to sit sentimentalizing, or mysticizing, are almost sure to become the prey of dark, black misgivings. John, struggling in the desert, needs no proof that Jesus is the Christ. John, shut up, becomes morbid and doubtful immediately. The history of a human soul is marvellous. We are mysterious; but here is the history of it all — for sadness, for suffering, for misgiving, there is no remedy but stirring and doing.

---

I resolve to neglect nothing to secure my eternal peace, more than if I had been certified that I should die within the day; nor to mind any thing which my secular duties demand of me, less than if I had been insured I should live fifty years more.

## HOW TO BE A MAN.

When Carlyle was asked by a young person to point out what course of reading he thought best to make him a man, he replied, in his characteristic manner, "It is not by books alone, or by books chiefly, that a man becomes in all points a man. Study to do faithfully whatsoever thing in your actual situation, then and now, you find either expressly or tacitly laid down to your charge — that is, stand to your post; stand in it like a true soldier. Silently devour the many chagrins of it, — all situations have many, — and see you aim not to quit it, without doing all that is your duty."

---

A CONTENTED HEART. — "I never complained of my condition," says the Persian poet Sadi, "but once, when my feet were bare, and I had no money to buy shoes; but I met a man without feet, and I became contented with my lot."

## CAUSES OF FAILURES IN BUSINESS.

The leading cause is an ambition to be rich; — by grasping too much, it defeats itself. Another cause is aversion to labor. The third cause is an impatient desire to enjoy the luxuries of life before the right to them has been at all acquired. Another cause arises from the want of some deeper principles for distinguishing between right and wrong than a reference merely to what is established as honorable in the society in which one happens to live.

---

Godly sorrow, like weeping Mary, seeks Christ; saving faith, like wrestling Jacob, finds and holds Christ; heavenly love, like the affectionate spouse, dwells with Christ, — it is an eternal grace, always lodging in the bosom of Christ. Lord, thou art the desire of my soul; O, that I could see thee, find and love thee, that I may forever enjoy thee!

## SELECTIONS FROM SCRIPTURE.

"ALL things work together for good to them that love God."

"Let him know, that he which converteth the sinner from the error of his way, shall save a soul from death, and shall hide a multitude of sins." — *James* v. 20.

"The Lord encampeth about them that love him."

"Be careful what you say, do, or think; God knows it all."

"If the righteous are scarcely saved, where shall the sinner and the ungodly appear?"

"Be not troubled about much serving; remember Christ's words to Martha."

"Exhort one another daily, while it is called to-day." — *Heb.* iii. 13.

"All things are naked and open unto the eyes of Him with whom we have to do." — *Heb.* iv. 13.

"Seeing then we have a great High Priest,

that is passed into the heavens, Jesus, the Son of God, let us hold fast our profession."

"Let us therefore come boldly unto the throne of grace, that we may obtain mercy, and find grace to help in time of need."

"Therefore to him that knoweth to do good, and doeth it not, to him it is sin." — *James* iv. 17.

"Humble yourselves in the sight of the Lord, and he shall lift you up."

"Think it not strange concerning the fiery trial which is to try you as though some strange thing happened unto you."

"For what shall it profit a man, if he shall gain the whole world and lose his own soul? or, what shall a man give in exchange for his soul?"

Reader, you will find it profitable to take the Bible and read the following: —

Mark xi. 24, 26.

Luke xviii. 17, 42; xix. 6, 9.

John v. 28, 29; x. 1, 9; xi. 25, 26; xii. 1, 3, 26; xiv. 3, 6, 12, 23; xv. 1, 18; xvi. 23, 33; xvii.

Acts x.
2 Cor. v. 10; vii. 10.
Ephesians iv. 30, 32.
Heb. iv. 12, 13; xiii. 16.
Matt. vii. 21, 23, 24.
Psalm xci.
Matt. xviii. 35; xix. 27, 30.
James i. 2, 3, 4, 5, 6, 12, 17; ii. 22, 24; iv. 8, 10.
1 Peter ii. 23, 24, 25; iii. 8, 13; iv. 8, 12, 13, 18.
1 John ii.; iii; iv.; v.
St. Mark i. 24, 25, 26.
Ephes. vi. 8, 18.
1 Cor. x. 1, 12.
Heb. xiii. 16.
James i. 27; iv. 8, 10, 17; v. 10, 11, 13, 16, 17.
1 Peter iii. 12, 15.
1 John ii.
1 John v.
Luke v. and vi.

## A SHORT SERMON ON MANLINESS.

Learn from the earliest days to insure your principles against the peril of ridicule. You can no more exercise your reason if you live in the constant dread of laughter, than you can enjoy your life if you are in the constant terror of death. If you think it right to differ from the times, and to make a point of morals, do it, however rustic, however antiquated, however pedantic it may appear; do it, not for insolence, but seriously and grandly, as a man who wore a soul of his own in his bosom, and did not wait till it was breathed into him by the breath of fashion.

---

Early Rising on the Sabbath.— Rise up *early* in the morning on the *Sabbath day*. Be careful to rise sooner on this day than on other days, by how much the service of God is to be preferred before all earthly business.

## TREES AND FLOWERS.

> Not a tree,
> A plant, a leaf, a blossom, but contains
> A folio volume. We may read, and read,
> And read again, and still find something new;
> Something to please and something to instruct,
> Even in the humble weed.

---

POINTED REPLY.— The Duke of Wellington, who had resided in the East, was gravely asked by a young clergyman, "Does not your grace think it almost useless and extravagant to preach the gospel to the Hindoos?" The Duke immediately rejoined, "Look, sir, to your marching orders, 'Preach the gospel to every creature.'"— *Mark* xvi. 15.

WHAT a marvellous gospel is that which opens a free portal to friendship with God for every sinner who will! and into which, if any sinner enter, he will find purification as well as peace!

## THINK.

Thought engenders thought. Place one idea upon paper, another will follow it, and still another, until you have written a page. You cannot fathom your mind. There is a well of thought there which has no bottom. The more you draw from it, the more clear and fruitful it will be. If you neglect to think yourself, and use other people's thoughts, giving them utterance only, you will never know what you are capable of. At first your ideas may come out in lumps, homely and shapeless; but no matter; time and perseverance will arrange and polish them. Learn to think, and you will learn to write; the more you think, the better you will express your ideas.

---

The best means of keeping near to God, is the closet. Here the battle is won or lost.

## WEAR A SMILE.

Which will you do, smile and make others happy, or be crabbed, and make every body round you miserable? You can live among beautiful flowers and singing birds, or in the mire surrounded by fogs and frogs. The amount of happiness which you can produce is incalculable, if you will show a smiling face, a kind heart, and speak pleasant words. On the other hand, by sour looks, cross words, and a fretful disposition, you can make hundreds unhappy almost beyond endurance. Which will you do? Wear a pleasant countenance, let joy beam in your eye, and love glow on your forehead. There is no joy so great as that which springs from a kind act or a pleasant deed, and you may feel it at night when you rest, and at morning when you rise, and through the day when about your daily business.

## DO GOOD.

Thousands of men breathe, move, and live, pass off the stage of life, and are heard of no more. Why? They did not a particle of good in the world; and none were blessed by them, none could point to them as the instruments of their redemption; not a word they spoke could be recalled, and so they perished; their light went out in darkness, and they were not remembered more than the insects of yesterday. Will you thus live and die, O man immortal? Live for something. Do good, and leave behind you a monument of virtue that the storm of time can never destroy. Write your name in kindness, love, and mercy; on the hearts of thousands you come in contact with year by year, and you will never be forgotten. No, your name, your deeds, will be as legible on the hearts you leave behind as the stars on the brow of evening. Good deeds will shine as the stars of heaven. — *Dr. Chalmers.*

## THE PREVENTION OF CRIME.

WHILE our legislature are about to pass statutes which affix penalties to certain crimes therein designated, will it not be well for our philanthropists to endeavor to stay the tide of vice which in so many cases leads to crime? In these matters we believe that "an ounce of prevention is worth a pound of cure," and while we would ask no relaxation of the remedial measures which society is forced to adopt for the preservation of order, we would, on the other hand, bespeak for the ignorant that care and watchfulness from society which will prevent their becoming criminals.

Society has done much for the young; but she has not performed her whole duty. There are thousands of children about our streets ill fed, poorly clad, and still more poorly educated. Their earliest breath is drawn in an atmosphere of penury, and their first companions are the idle and the unprincipled. When old enough to attend school, their parents have no means of making them appear decent, and the consequence is, they prowl about our streets and wharves, imbibing principles which are sure to lead to the commission of crime. When some of these children are temporarily induced to attend school, their low grade makes them objects of derision, and they fall back into their old practices for want of sympathy, encouragement, and support.

Now, we hold that before society inflicts penalties for the violation of law, upon the ground of a *moral right* to do so, she is in duty bound to wash her hands of being *particeps criminis* to the offence, by so educating her members as to negative this tendency to crime.

When we observe a parent neglecting the education of his children, we complain of the injury which he is likely to inflict upon society. But society stands, and must stand in *loco parentis*, to the children of the poor. Shall our city, then, suffer these poor children to grow up in ignorance and vice, and then punish them in their adult years for the crimes which have been induced by long and tedious years of poverty, suffering, and bad example?

It may be urged, and with truth, that many of these poor children are dependent upon their own exertions for support for themselves and their parents, and that therefore they cannot attend school. Granted. But we have schools on the Sabbath which they could attend. Is is urged that they have not proper clothing? Then let the benevolent look over their wardrobes, and let the ladies, ever sympathizing with human need, provide a depository where this clothing may be sent and recut, and make for these destitute children suitable garments for the purpose. It is humiliating to say it, but such is the fact, that the moths every summer devour twice as much cloth in the wardrobes of our citizens as would suffice to clothe all our poor population, and it only requires a little energy to divert this clothing into a channel where it would be useful.

But again it is urged that the poorer children

cannot be made to assemble on Sundays at the Sabbath school. This is not true. If these children were properly clothed and treated with kindness by the teachers and pupils, thousands would be rescued every year from a life of vice and immorality. The experiment is worth trying, and we are confident that the cost thereof would save our city thousands of dollars in remedial measures for crime, and the result would be to secure to the movers the blessings of the poor for generations to come. Shall not the experiment be tried?

---

INTOXICATING DRINKS. — President Jefferson once said, " The habit of using ardent spirits by men in office has occasioned more injury to the public, and more trouble to me, than all other causes. And were I to commence my administration again, with the experience I now have, the first question I would ask respecting a candidate would be, ' Does he use ardent spirits?' "

## GOD KNOWS IT ALL.

In the dim recess of thy spirit's chamber,
  Is there some hidden grief thou mayst not tell?
Let not thy heart forsake thee; but remember,
  His pitying eye, who sees and knows it well,
            God knows it all!


And art thou tossed on billows of temptation,
  And wouldst do good, but evil oft prevails?
O think, amid the waves of tribulation,
  When earthly hopes and earthly refuge fails,
            God knows it all!


And dost thou sin, thy deed of shame concealing
  In some dark spot no human eye can see,
Then walk in pride, without one sigh revealing
  The deep remorse that should disquiet thee?
            God knows it all!


Art thou oppressed, and poor, and heavy-hearted,
  The heavens above thee in thick clouds arrayed,
And well-nigh crushed, no earthly thought imparted,
  No friendly voice to say, "Be not afraid?"
            God knows it all!

Art thou a mourner? Are thy tear-drops flowing
  For one too early lost to earth and thee?
The depths of grief no human spirit knowing,
  Which moan in secret, like the moaning sea?
        God knows it all!

Dost thou look back upon a life of sinning?
  Forward, and tremble for thy future lot?
There's One who sees the end from the beginning, —
  Thy tear of penitence is unforgot, —
        God knows it all!

Then go to God. Pour out your hearts before him;
  There is no grief your Father cannot feel;
And let your grateful songs of praise adore him, —
  To save, forgive, and every wound to heal.
        God knows it all — God knows it all!

---

CHARACTER. — As they who, for every slight infirmity, take physic to repair their health, do rather impair it, so they who, for every trifle, are eager to vindicate their character, do rather weaken it.

## HOW TO LIVE.

He liveth long who liveth well!
  All other life is short and vain:
He liveth longest who can tell
  Of living most for heavenly gain.

He liveth long who liveth well!
  All else is being flung away;
He liveth longest who can tell
  Of true things truly done each day.

Waste not thy being; back to him
  Who freely gave it, freely give;
Else is that being but a dream;
  'Tis but to *be*, and not to *live*.

Be what thou seemest! live thy creed!
  Hold up to earth the torch divine;
Be what thou prayest to be made;
  Let the great Master's steps be thine.

Fill up each hour with what will last;
  Buy up the moments as they go:
The life above, when this is past,
  Is the ripe fruit of life below.

Sow truth, if thou the true wouldst reap;
　Who sows the false shall reap the vain;
Erect and sound thy conscience keep;
　From hollow words and deeds refrain.

Sow love, and taste its fruitage pure;
　Sow peace, and reap its harvests bright;
Sow sunbeams on the rock and moor,
　And find a harvest-home of light.

---

A LADY who had refused to give, after hearing a charity sermon, had her pocket picked as she was leaving the church. On making the discovery, she said, "God could not find the way into my pocket, but it seems the devil did."

THE venerable church of Saint Mark, at Venice, is to be thoroughly repaired, and it is proposed to modernize the ancient clock, which, like all old Italian timepieces, has a dial plate which shows the hours from 1 to 24, instead of from 1 to 12.

## THE GOLDEN CITY.

### BY REV. EDWIN H. NEVIN.

I SEE the Golden City
  With towers standing high;
Its walls of sparkling beauty
  Are shining in the sky.

Its pearly gates are open —
  . Are open night and day;
And through them all are shining
  A light that cheers my way.

I hear its rich-toned music
  Come pealing through the air;
It flows o'er hill and valley,
  It soundeth every where.

In it my friends are gathered,
  The loved ones gone before;
They're robed in angel beauty,
  On angel wings they soar.

Within the Golden City
  I hope to fly and sing,
And sound the praise forever
  Of Christ, my Lord and King.

>     Forever and forever
>       That city shall be mine,
>     The lovely, Golden City,
>       Which does the sun outshine.

---

HINTS TO CHRISTIANS. — The way to secure the future, is to improve the present.

Opportunities to do good create obligations to do it; he that hath the means must answer for the end.

Prefer the duty you owe to the danger you fear.

A CLERGYMAN who recently visited Malaga, Madrid, Seville, and Cadiz, to ascertain whether copies of the Bible may be freely introduced there, reports that he found a general desire to possess the Scriptures, and great facilities for distributing them.

## PRAYER.

" PRAY without ceasing." — 1 *Thess.* v. 17.

> "Prayer was appointed to convey
> The blessings God designs to give;
> Long as they live should Christians pray,
> For only while they pray they live."
>
> *Hart.*

" Prayer is a retirement from earth to attend on God, and hold correspondence with him that dwells in heaven. The things of the world, therefore, must be commanded to stand by for a season, and to abide at the foot of the mount, while we walk up higher to offer up our sacrifices, as Abraham did, and to meet our God." — *Watts.*

> " In every storm, that either frowns or falls,
> What an asylum has the soul in prayer!"
>
> *Young.*

" In the absence of the sun, the mild and peaceful radiance of the moon enlivens our path. Let devotion spread a cheering light over your darkest hours. 'The Queen of Night,' says Bowdler, 'unveils its full beauty when the hours of joy and lustre have passed away, pouring, as it were, a holy light through the damps and darkness of adversity.' Thus will constant prayer cheer the darkest season of affliction." — *Bickersteth.*

"In this valley of sorrow and strife,
  Prayer shall rise with my earliest breath;
It shall mix in the business of life,
  And soften the struggles of death."

*Cunningham.*

"As the hart panteth after the water brooks, so panteth my soul after thee, O God. When shall I come and appear before God." — *David.*

"Prayer is the most secret intercourse of the soul with God; and, as it were, the conversation of one heart with another." — *Dr. A. Clark.*

"A little girl, about four years of age, being asked, 'Why do you pray to God?' replied,

'Because I know he hears me, and I love to pray to him.' 'But how do you know he hears you?' Putting the little hand to her heart, she said, 'I know he does, because there is something *here* that tells me so.'" — *Arvine's Cyclopædia.*

"Angels are round the good man, to catch the incense of his prayers; and they fly to minister kindness to those for whom he pleadeth." — *Tupper.*

"Prayer is not eloquence, but earnestness; not the definition of helplessness, but the feeling of it; not figures of speech, but compunction of soul." — *Hannah More.*

> "O thou, by whom we come to God,
> The Life, the Truth, the Way,
> The path of prayer thyself hast trod;
> Lord, teach us how to pray."
>
> *Montgomery.*

"Is any among you afflicted? let him pray." — *James* v. 13.

## WHITEFIELD'S EXPERIENCE.

"My mind being now more enlarged, I began to read the Holy Scriptures upon my knees, laying aside all other books, and praying over, if possible, every line and word. This proved meat indeed, and drink indeed, to my soul. I daily received fresh life, light, and power from above. I got more true knowledge from reading the Book of God in one month, than I could ever have acquired from all the writings of men. In one word, I found it profitable for reproof, for correction, for instruction; every way sufficient to make the man of God perfect, thoroughly furnished for every good work and word. About this time God was pleased to enlighten my soul, and bring me into the knowledge of his free grace, and the necessity of being justified in his sight by faith only. Burkitt's and Henry's Expositions were of admirable use to lead me into this and all other gospel truths."

To these habits of reading, Whitefield added much secret prayer. "O, what sweet communion had I daily vouchsafed with God in prayer! How often have I been carried out beyond myself when meditating in the fields! How assuredly I felt that Christ dwelt in me and I in him, and how, daily, did I walk in the comforts of the Holy Ghost, and was edified and refreshed in the multitude of peace!"

---

DURATION OF LIFE. — The duration of man's life should not be estimated by his years, but by what he has accomplished — by the uses which he has made of time and opportunity. The industrious man lives longer than the drone; and by inuring our body and mind to exercise and activity, we shall more than double the years of our existence.

## A WORD FROM OLD SOUTH CHAPEL.

A HISTORY of the jailer's conversion at Philippi was read as the lesson of the morning. The prayers of Paul and Silas induced God to send an earthquake to convince the jailer of sin.

A young brother, who was converted last Saturday, stood up and testified to the grace of God that had been revealed to his soul.

Dr. Pease stated that he had been several weeks laboring in a town near the head of the Connecticut River, where there has been no conversion for fifty years. God has now begun the work of conversion. Several heads of families have pledged themselves to serve the Lord Jesus Christ. One man, a rumseller, who has done much to pollute the morals of the town, has abandoned the traffic and come over on the Lord's side. This place has especially been remembered in the prayers at the Old South Chapel.

The tidings from the neighborhood meetings in the city were very encouraging. The gospel is being preached to the poor with glorious success.

It was stated that two sailors were converted last evening. One sailor has just returned from a voyage who was converted a few months ago. He has returned in health and soul prosperity.

One young man arose and said that he had lately found peace in believing. Another brother stated that about one year since he was in this room, and received such impressions as issued in his conversion.

A brother from Western New York stated that this meeting was exerting a great influence upon the world. He has seen a sailor who was converted, that received his first impressions in this meeting. He said, also, that he had met persons through all the West who had received their first impressions in this chapel.

The aisles and gallery were all filled, and the meeting is highly encouraging.

## EVERY MAN'S LIFE A PLAN OF GOD.

Every human soul has a complete and perfect plan, cherished for it in the heart of God; a divine biography marked out, which it enters into life, to live. This life, rightfully unfolded, will be a complete and beautiful whole; an experience led on by God and unfolded by the secret nurture of the world; a drama cast in the mould of a perfect art, with no part wanting, a divine study for the man himself, and for others; a study that shall forever unfold, in wondrous beauty, the love and faithfulness of God; great in its conception, great in the divine skill by which it is shaped; above all, great in the momentous and glorious issues it prepares. What a thought is this for every human soul to cherish! What dignity does it add to life! What support does it bring to the trials of life! What instigation does it add to send us on in every thing that constitutes our excellence! We live in the divine thought.

We fill a place in the great, everlasting plan of God's intelligence. We never sink below his care — never drop out of his counsel. —*Dr. Bushnell.*

THE MOST IMPORTANT THOUGHT. — " I want you to tell me," said a gentleman to the late distinguished Mr. Webster, " What is the most important thought that ever occupied your mind?" " The most important thought that ever occupied my mind," said Mr. Webster, with the deepest seriousness, " was that of *my individual responsibility to God.*"

A WORD TO MOTHERS. — If the time that is spent by mothers in places of amusement should be spent in narrating to children the history of the Bible, we should soon have jails and prisons to let.

Contrast the feelings of two mothers on a dying bed. One left a son, a successful minister of the gospel; he studied theology beside a pious mother, commencing at the age of five.

The other, left a son in prison for life; he was educated in the street, and in grog-shops, while his mother was in places of amusement!

A young man presented himself before a committee as a candidate for the ministry. He was asked, who he studied theology with? his answer was, My mother! They wanted no better evidence of his piety.

Mothers, remember the young man that wrote with a piece of chalk on his prison wall the *five steps to the gallows.* Learn your children (commencing at the age of five) to write on their hearts the five steps to the paradise of God.

## CONCLUSION.

SEARCH the Bible and this book daily. It will enable you to see the great object of this life, which is to do good to others, and to love and glorify God, and prepare to meet him in heaven. Burn up your novels, and give up your places of amusement; and attend the prayer-meeting; it will learn you the way to do good to others, which is a foretaste of heavenly things: for who is more happy than he that is doing good to others?

Take the example of Rev. Mr. Cleveland, the City Missionary of Boston. A gentleman taking him by the hand, with these words, " Sir, you are a happy man." " Yes, I am a happy man; for who can be more so than he who is trying to make others happy." While you are doing good to others, you are transported with delight by the prospect of the happy land, where no one says he is sick; and when the hour of death arrives, and the spirit leaves this body of clay, it leaves all worldly thoughts with it, and becomes brilliant and active, and ready to receive the great mystery of godliness. You are transported on angelic wings to the pearly gates of the New Jerusalem, where you are welcomed into the golden city by that angelic throng that sang praises at the time you gave your heart to God. " There is more joy by the angels in heaven over one sinner that repenteth, than over ninety and nine just persons that need no repentance." Christ presents you here a crown of rejoicing. You see the place he prepared for you, eighteen hundred years ago; you behold "the tree that bears its twelve manner of fruit," and "the river of water pure as crystal;" "the mystery of godliness begins to unfold; you are satisfied." "I shall be satisfied when I awake with thy likeness." — Psal. xvii. 15. Is this to be eternal? We can count the sands upon the sea-shore, but not the years of eternity. Trusting in the Lord that you have made your final decision to obtain the everlasting crown — WE BID YOU ALL GOD-SPEED.

THE END.

www.ingramcontent.com/pod-product-compliance
Lightning Source LLC
Chambersburg PA
CBHW030427300426
44112CB00009B/890